DAN SHEEHAN

FOREWORD BY JONATHAN SHAY, MD, PHD

CONTINUING ACTIONS

A WARRIOR'S GUIDE TO COMING HOME

— ALSO BY DAN SHEEHAN —

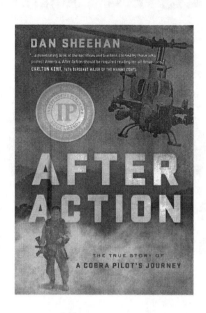

AFTER ACTION:
THE TRUE STORY OF A COBRA PILOT'S JOURNEY

IndieReader Discovery Award, 2015, Memoir

Gold Medal, 2014 Independent Publisher Book Awards, Memoir

Silver Medal, 2014 Military Writers Society of America, Memoir

Bronze Medal, 2014 Independent Publisher Book Awards, E-Book

"In this sensitive and intensely presented memoir, Sheehan addresses his tours of duty during the Iraq War and the burdens he grappled with as a result. His vivid prose conveys the turmoil and danger of piloting a combat helicopter and the special psychology of fighting, but his real story lies in dealing with the return to 'normal' life. . . .

Sheehan's writing and recommendations deserve the attention of anyone interested in this important issue, which is as topical as tomorrow's headlines."

—*Publishers Weekly Select* (starred review)

"AFTER ACTION is not for those sensitive to profanity or depictions of real bloodshed. However, it provides a remarkable window into the experiences of combat pilots and the mindset of soldiers." —*IndieReader*

". . . excellent book on several levels. Sense-stirring descriptions of air combat . . . camaraderie of pilots comes across well . . . Adroit use of interior monologue enhances many pulsating scenes and puts the reader . . . in the head of the author pilot."

—*21st Annual Writer's Digest Self-Published Book Awards*

". . . vividly portrays the details of external and internal carnage that transpire when a human assumes the role of warrior and 'bears the burden of peace.' Well-paced action and reflective insight balance out into an incredible read. . . .

. . . AFTER ACTION has my highest recommendation. It is a remarkable human battle story and a healing tool."

—*Military Writers Society of America*

Continuing Actions:
A Warrior's Guide To Coming Home

©2015 by Dan Sheehan

ISBN: 978-1-5171805-1-5

Editorial development and creative design support by Ascent:
www.itsyourlifebethere.com

Design by Peter Gloege | LOOK Design Studio

Follow Dan Sheehan:
www.DanSheehanAuthor.com
 (search) Dan Sheehan Author   @dansheehan_dan

To the generations of veterans who've come before me:
Your hard work, sacrifice, and suffering
set the stage for my successful return from combat.
Thank you.

WHAT IS TO

GIVE LIGHT MUST

ENDURE BURNING.

—VIKTOR E. FRANKL

FOREWORD by Dr. Jonathan Shay 9

PROLOGUE 19

PART ONE:
THE WARRIOR'S JOURNEY—WHAT WE DON'T KNOW

1 NONE OF THIS IS NEW 29

2 DEADLY MISCONCEPTIONS 45

3 THE MYTHIC POWER OF WAR 61

4 SOCIETY'S ROLE 71

5 THE VALUE OF MYTH 81

PART TWO:
COMPLETING THE WARRIOR'S JOURNEY

6 GETTING PHYSICAL 101

7 EMOTIONS, SHIT 123

8 KUM BAY YAH, ANYONE? 137

9 LOOK AT IT 151

10 "DOC!" 165

PART THREE:
DUTY

11 AS UNSELFISH AS IT GETS 185

EPILOGUE 201

CONCLUSION 207

ACKNOWLEDGEMENTS 211

BIBLIOGRAPHY 213

ADDITIONAL SUGGESTED READING 215

APPENDIX A 217

APPENDIX B 221

APPENDIX C 223

FOREWORD

by JONATHAN SHAY, MD, PhD

(Foreword copyright, 2015, by Jonathan Shay[1])

THIS FOREWORD REFLECTS my appreciation and respect for both this book and Dan Sheehan's earlier, *After Action*. Both books are vividly and energetically written with a wealth of striking explanatory metaphors, such as describing the life-saving suppression of all emotions that do not *directly* contribute to surviving in war as a tourniquet. A tourniquet may be life-saving in the needful moment, but limbs die and become gangrenous if it is left on too long. Carrying the tourniquet of suppression and compartmentalization of emotions back to civilian life has ruined the health and happiness of countless veterans and their families.

I especially applaud Sheehan for his emphasis on *sleep*. Sleep is an essential logistical entity that gets used up and must be resupplied—just like water, fuel, and ammo—and for which no amount of good attitude and motivation can substitute.[2] This is especially true during *recovery* from combat and combat trauma. *Every* wellness discipline—yes, medicine—but also psychology, acupuncture, chiropractic, massage, clinical hypnosis, prayer, and meditation has a toolbag for sleep. Sheehan is persistent,

---

[1] This Foreword is licensed without fee to Dan Sheehan for publication with his book *Continuing Actions*, in its entirety, but may not be republished separately from it elsewhere, except by permission of the copyright holder, Jonathan Shay.

[2] Shay, J., "Ethical Standing for Commander Self-Care: The Need For Sleep." Parameters: U.S. Army War College Quarterly, 28:93-105, Summer 1998. http://strategicstudiesinstitute.army.mil/pubs/parameters/Articles/98summer/shay.htm

practical, and persuasive on attention to sleep as a requirement if one is to make a healthy and successful return to civilian life, or life in garrison, after going to war. In my decades of clinical work with veterans, I have found adequate, restorative sleep to be the single most powerful predictor of a flourishing life after return from war.

It is well known that combat trauma murders sleep. But dangerously less well known is the fact that the cheapest, most easily available "medicine" for sleep—alcohol—also murders sleep. After return from war, combat veterans are frequently desperate to fall asleep and turn to alcohol, because, initially at least, it works. The trouble is, it burns off way too fast and you wake up too soon. Then the logic at 2 am is irresistible: "If two shots got me to sleep, two more will get me *back to sleep* . . . ." At the risk of getting too technical, acute tolerance sets in so fast that it's demonstrable even with one dose. Couple this with withdrawal syndrome—the flip side of tolerance—and you wake up (too soon) even more wired (a mini-withdrawal) than when you went to sleep. This is one of the quickest ways to find yourself on the icy stairway to alcohol dependence and abuse. Satan is not part of my normal vocabulary, but I say without embarrassment as a psychopharmacologist: The pharmacology of alcohol with respect to sleep was designed by Satan himself.

The subtitle of my first book, *Achilles in Vietnam*, is "*Combat Trauma and the Undoing of Character.*" In it I introduced and explored the concept of "moral injury" and observed that moral injury can deteriorate good character to the point where a good person turns bad. The whole of the story of Achilles in Homer's *Iliad* is a story of moral injury and its awful consequences, mainly for other people. My definition of moral injury consists of three components: **1.** A betrayal of "what's right" **2.** by someone holding legitimate authority 3. in a high-stakes situation. This is NOT the story that Dan Sheehan tells of himself in his two books. He did have expert, ethical, and properly supported leadership that did not betray him. But he did not escape combat unscathed.

He took a blow of a sort that I discussed in *Achilles in Vietnam* under the rather opaque term used by ethical philosophers, "moral luck," meaning moral *bad* luck. Navy psychiatrist William Nash, along with a substantial group of clinical psychologists-researchers at the National Center for PTSD—most notably, Shira Maguen, Brett Litz, and Kent Drescher—and others have used the term "moral injury" as a synonym for bad moral luck. They use the same 1-2-3 structure, but with a crucially different second term: 2. "I did it. I betrayed what's right."[3] Bad moral luck is a situation where *none* of the available alternatives for action leave you clean, and even taking the "right" action causes moral injury. Sheehan's pain-laden syllogism, "Good people don't kill. I killed. What does that make me?" *(After Action, p.318)* is the voice of this second form of moral injury.

Both flavors of moral injury impair the capacity for trust and both are fertile soil for the growth of *despair*—the settled conviction that "*I* am no longer capable of virtue!" People in despair willingly end their own lives. It is a state of pain comparable to the suffering of those in intense paranoid states, which are also fertile soil for suicide. Some psychodynamically inclined mental health professionals hold that paranoia is a "defense" against shame and despair. Both are hideous states of pain and both are drivers of suicide.

Both forms of moral injury are real and both are important.

---

[3] Georgetown University Philosopher Nancy Sherman assures me that discussions of good moral luck do exist, but they are not easy to find.

If I am riveted by the form of moral injury that requires leadership malpractice in its definition, it is because **prevention** of psychological and moral injury in military service has become the focus of my life's work. Improving upon the average level of functional expertise and ethical performance by American troop leaders is visibly within our grasp—if we remove the toxic effects of careerism on both the functional expertise and ethical performance of military leaders. Explaining how to accomplish this is a book unto itself, so I shall just assert that significant cultural change is needed in our military if we are to move beyond simply *treating* moral injury and learn to *prevent* it.

Continuing Actions has the best portrait of the workings of **workaholism** in the life of a combat veteran that I have ever read or heard (including my own in *Odysseus in America*). This is the most common strategy that veterans use, and many find it hard to consider this a product of psychological injury. This is because steady, successful work brings home bushels of money—the very definition of doing well in our society. "He (or she) is rolling in dough—he must be okay!" The problem is, workaholic veterans overlook bringing one big thing home from work—themselves. A common pattern is that they start each day sleep deprived and exhausted, work two or three jobs in succession, and maybe stop off for a drink or two before returning home and flopping exhaustedly into the recliner, sofa, or bed to sleep badly. Then the alarm goes off and they do it all again. They might be earning money, but this "okay" veteran is at risk for losing his or her job, family, and life.

There is a common, yet dangerous, misconception many veterans have that they must meet the full clinical diagnosis of PTSD before their psychological injury is legitimate and worthy of treatment. This leads many to ignore their injuries until they become overwhelming—often ruining their lives in the process. *Continuing Actions* is not written in clinical language, although some terms are unavoidable, and Sheehan has done an admirable job translating the technical jargon of human psychology into terms and metaphors all veterans can appreciate. Sheehan's voice is that of a proud Marine veteran, and the personal details from his own life clearly show the insidious impact a psychological injury can have if left unattended.

I prefer to speak of psychological injury, rather than "PTSD." PTSD is part of the official classification of mental disorders by the American Psychiatric Association (APA) and is not a bad summary of what it looks like when you have been in a situation where other human beings were trying to kill you and you have survived. PTSD is a summary of the adaptations that let you survive that threat, but *that persist after the danger has passed*. I and many others, including General Pete Chiarelli, former Army Vice Chief of Staff, have begged the APA to simply substitute the word "injury" for "disorder" as less stigmatizing in military culture. The reasons for this are not obvious to civilians. To be injured in the service of one's country is entirely honorable. To fall ill, to get a disease or disorder, are not *dis*honorable, but they sure are *unlucky*. Nobody wants to share a fighting hole with an unlucky infantryman, a ship's watch with an unlucky sailor, or an aircraft with an unlucky aviator. To be unlucky *is* stigmatizing in that culture.

I prefer the term "psychological injury" as the broadest umbrella term to name changes in the mind, body, spirit, and character as a result of bad experience. So for me, PTSD is one form of psychological injury, not the whole ball of wax.

Continuing Actions carries a credible message of hope to veterans laboring forward under a burden of psychological and moral injury: "What if you got back a long time ago and have been stationary ever since? Have you missed your opportunity to successfully return home? Absolutely not. It doesn't matter how long you've stagnated—minutes or decades—the road ahead remains open to you." People have asked me, "Is recovery from PTSD possible?"—using the sloppy popular umbrella term for *everything* that can go wrong in the mind and spirit as a result of going to war. I simply reply that I have seen it happen. As William of Ockham said in the 14th century, "What is—is possible!"

Dan Sheehan draws on the shared culture of today's military service members when he introduces "echelons" of wound care—in this case, psychological and moral injury—as self-aid, buddy-aid, and corpsman-aid. Remember—Sheehan was a Marine so he uses "corpsman" where the Army and Air Force use "medic." This concept of taking care of injuries at the lowest level possible is missing from our treatment of psychological injuries. Instead, veterans often allow relatively minor psychological injuries to remain untreated until massive clinical interventions are required to even stabilize, let alone heal, them. This places tremendous strain on limited mental health resources and degrades the care available to those whose injuries demand immediate clinical attention. The only way to fix the problem of too many veterans seeking help too late is to expand the treatment of psychological injuries outside the clinician's office—and to encourage veterans to deal with them early.

One of the giants of the psychological trauma field, Judith Herman, has taught that the foundation of recovery from trauma is safety, sobriety, and self-care. While her great trauma program at Cambridge Health Alliance has always offered and encouraged peer-based group programs for its trauma survivors, I'm not sure she ever fully "got" the indispensable role of peers—"buddy-aid"—when the psychologically and morally injured are service members and veterans. This is entirely understandable, given the institutional ecology of a place like the Boston-Cambridge area, where there are four VA medical centers with attendant outpatient clinics within commuting distance. These vacuum up most of the Boston area veterans so she didn't have on-the-ground clinical experience with them. I applaud Sheehan's use of Herman's *Trauma and Recovery* as a resource in *Continuing Actions,* even though I find Dr. Herman's material on veterans to be rather thin compared with her material on the other trauma populations she discusses. I owe her, and her co-founder at Cambridge Health Alliance, Mary Harvey, PhD, immeasurable debts as teachers and mentors, and can only hope that they are proud of my productive use of their teachings in a different territory. Their footprints are all over my brain.

In fairness, having inhabited the Boston VA ecology myself for 20 years, I would not say that the VA as a whole and as a culture really embraces the concept of buddy-aid, either—being wedded as it is to the cultural prestige and grandeur of *credentialed professionals* such as myself. VA mental health offers many "group therapies," but instinctively reacts to real cohesion among veterans in the groups the way the owners of non-union businesses react to real cohesion among employees—fearful they might turn against "management." This may partially explain the VA's overwhelming preference for rigidly structured, "manualized" group therapies. But real cohesion is a combat-strength multiplier in military forces, and Sheehan offers pragmatic suggestions for how to carry such cohesion into the veteran community.

Let me explain: The key resources needed to prevent psychological and moral injury are: **cohesion**—positive qualities of community in the face-to-face unit, including its direct leaders, and *stability* is crucial for this; **leadership**—expert, ethical, and properly supported from above/below; and **training**—prolonged, cumulative, and highly realistic for what people actually have to do and face. These are three concrete, actionable, and measurable dimensions of trust within military units. They are demonstrably combat-strength multipliers, and equally, are protective against psychological and moral injury. Wow! Combat effectiveness and mental health force protection in one package—Yes! The uniformed and civilian leadership of any military force ought to be drooling at the chance to do it.

I shall spare the reader my rant on this US Armed Forces *akrasia* [a philosophical term meaning, "Knowing the right thing to do, but doing something else instead"], which cannot be fully cured by the uniformed or civilian leadership of the Armed Forces alone. The Congress must reform the Officer Personnel Act of 1947, and all its weakling progeny. Similarly, only the Congress can increase the end-strength of the Forces, so that the deployment tempo and the operating tempo do not *inevitably* destroy beneficial policies on sleep budgets, both during deployment and when training-up at home station. I recall sitting in the cubicle of a one-star working for my boss, the Army Deputy Chief of Staff for Personnel, in 2004 or 2005. I said, "You folks *must* ask Congress for an increase in end strength. You are just burning through the forces, and the Guard and Reserves are already about destroyed by this OPTEMPO." My interlocutor cocked his head in the direction of Secretary of Defense Rumsfeld's office and said, "They'll never agree to that!" At the time, I held the grand title, "Chair of Ethics, Leadership, and Personnel Policy in the Office of the Army Deputy Chief of Staff for Personnel."

Prevention of psychological and moral injury in military service remains the fire in my belly. Until the tectonic plates of military bureaucracy and Congress shift enough to accommodate the baseline requirements for prevention, however, our veterans will continue to come home from war bearing psychological injuries. If that shift ever happens, the advice contained in *Continuing Actions* can be safely shelved. Until then, read on.

Jonathan Shay, MD, PhD was a VA psychiatrist for 20 years, working exclusively with psychologically and morally injured Vietnam combat veterans, who, he says, "kidnapped me and made me their missionary on prevention of psychological and moral injury to the Armed Forces, the Congress and the public." Dr. Shay performed the *Commandant of the Marine Corps Trust Study (1999-2000)*; held the Chair of Ethics, Leadership, and Personnel Policy for the Army Staff (2004-2005); and was the Omar Bradley Chair of Strategic Leadership at the US Army War College (Spring Semester, 2009). He was also a MacArthur Fellow (2008-2012). He is the author of *Achilles in Vietnam: Combat Trauma and the Undoing of Character* and of *Odysseus in America: Combat Trauma and the Trials of Homecoming*, with Foreword jointly by US Senators John McCain and Max Cleland. He is currently working on a third book in his ancient Greek's "franchise" on the military and veteran connections and the functions of classical Athenian tragedy.

PROLOGUE

FODDER IS A GOOD FRIEND and former squadron mate of mine. But being good friends does nothing to shield me from his caustic wit—in fact, just the opposite. Among other, unprintable, things he used to welcome me to work with a loud "You should have told me it was ugly shirt day—I would have worn mine, too!" Friendships among warriors are like that.

Every squadron ready-room, squad bay, and police station briefing-room has someone like Fodder. If they're lucky, two or three. Forget your hand-held radio? They'll put it in the freezer in a block of ice. Screw up on a flight or training exercise? They immediately roast you in a cartoon on the dry-erase board. In normal, peacetime life, they are stress-relievers. In combat, they are lifesavers.

Using humor as a shield, we who are warriors keep our minds, and everyone else's, firmly focused on the superficial. Driving a police car in Chicago, flying a Predator over Afghanistan, or on a foot patrol in Ramadi are not places to get distracted by profound thoughts. In those situations, and countless others, it is imperative that the mind remains on the immediate surface level of life. Our survival depends on it.

When I first told Fodder I was writing this book to help veterans, he was characteristically blunt. "Let me get this straight. You're writing a self-help book for folks who don't like self-help books, to help them overcome a problem they don't want to admit they have. Good plan. Let me know how that goes." Humor, a slight put-down, and then on to something else—classic Fodder.

He might have just been poking fun at me, but his response highlights the reason why, in the face of his logical critique of this book's premise, I chose to write it anyway.

This was a tough choice because I'm not normally a "Hey, you need to do this" kind of guy. I much prefer minding my own business and letting others take care of theirs. But Fodder's immediate negative reaction to the idea that there is anything we, as veterans, need to address after coming home made me realize that I had to step out of my comfort zone. It wasn't enough to just take care of myself anymore.

I've spent the last ten years navigating my own return from combat and have learned valuable lessons along the way. But these lessons don't just apply to me. They're applicable to many, if not most, veterans after they come home. The simple fact that I had to learn them by trial and error betrays a gap in our understanding of the challenges of service that few of us even know exists.

This gap becomes apparent when our battles are over because, for as much as we know about combat, modern warriors don't know shit about coming home.

As members of dangerous, sometimes deadly professions, our training has encouraged us to remain on the surface level of life. It's safer there because banter, humor, and bravado protect us from the dehumanizing effects of what we must do in the line of duty. But remaining on this superficial level exacts a heavy toll.

Even if we ignored the profound impact of our combat experiences, we did not pass through them unscathed. The events we've lived through, and the life-altering decisions we've made in milliseconds, have changed us at a fundamental level—whether we acknowledge it or not.

We've watched friends die, taken lives ourselves, and

experienced emotions ranging from terror to elation in less than a heartbeat. The randomness of indirect fire, the carnage of an IED going off in a crowded street, and the crushing anguish of civilians caught in the crossfire all stay with us long after the fact.

That we would encounter such soul-jarring things is not unexpected. They are part and parcel of the warrior's journey we embarked upon when we decided to serve in the first place. We trained to compartmentalize our intense reactions and became masters at stuffing them away. Our training kept us focused amid chaos and carnage, and, as long as we did what we'd been taught, things turned out fine. But then we came home.

Home—the magical place we fantasized about. The place where, if we could just get back to it, everything would be all right. Promises of carefree living, happy times with family and friends, and dreams of idyllic perfection invaded our thoughts while we were overseas. Even if we knew they were just dreams, they shaped our expectations and, by the time we finally did come home, we expected them to be true. Walking through that door was to be the end of our journey, the final act we had to accomplish as warriors and the gateway to the rest of our lives.

But that's not how it went.

Instead of carefree happiness we found unease. Instead of moving into the future, we became anchored in the past. Unexpected reactions came at us from nowhere, and each day we grew farther from the person we wanted to be. Confused as to what was happening, we closed down, reverted to the tactics of combat, and mentally barricaded ourselves behind thick, protective berms.

Because we had not been warned that challenges adjusting to life back home are normal, we considered ourselves outliers, alone in having difficulty with something others appeared to breeze past. Our unexpected vulnerability hinted at weakness and became something to hide at all costs. Family and friends were kept at arm's length, not allowed in for fear they'd see what was hidden behind our bravado. Deployments tore holes in our relationships that didn't close when we came home. Instead, emotional separation picked up where the physical left off. Some relationships never recovered.

These responses are nothing to be ashamed of. In fact, most men and women experience them after combat. The unease and disconnectedness that has infiltrated our lives is normal for this phase of the warrior's journey—the phase where we've left the battlefield but it refuses to leave us. They are symptoms of an incomplete transformation, of being stranded somewhere between war and peace, and they tell us our journey is not over yet. But our understanding of what it means to be a warrior does not include ways to deal with these normal reactions. We don't know how to address them and, as a result, are exposed to unnecessary injury and our families to needless pain.

The warrior's journey is not a lark. It has very real consequences that go beyond the acknowledged physical dangers. This journey is a transformative one, and the person who finishes it is necessarily different from the one who started. We don't get to choose whether we are changed or not—only how we deal with it.

This journey offers, to one brave enough to descend below the superficial, a chance to mature and grow wiser. That's the goal of completing the warrior's journey—to learn from our extraordinary experiences and use that knowledge to continue to serve our families, our comrades, and our nation. Unfortunately we, as modern warriors, have not been prepared to *complete* the warrior's journey, only to begin it.

That's the aim of this book—to fill the gaps in our knowledge and assist veterans through the challenges of coming home. These challenges cannot be ignored, out-run, out-drank, or out-worked because avoidance only feeds their power to destroy us from within. Overcoming them demands just as much courage as combat or possibly more. But the rewards are worth it.

It is in this final phase of the warrior's journey where you gain understanding of how, and how deeply, your experiences have affected you. You'll learn how to quiet the leftover physical reactions of combat and what to do when waves of emotions come crashing down out of nowhere. You'll begin to dismantle the walls that protected you well in combat but are now liabilities. You'll gain the strength and confidence to let people into the haunted places in your memories and begin to close the emotional distance between you and those you love. You'll put aside the fears that you'll be judged, laughed at, or misunderstood and break the trap that has claimed the happiness of generations of veterans before you.

The Marine Corps Battle Skills Training Handbook (before it was re-named the Marine Corps Common Skills Handbook) defined continuing actions as "Those activities that remain in place throughout any military operation and as such contribute to minimizing the amount of friction a unit imposes on itself." These aren't sexy, fun, or exciting jobs—hygiene, keeping your personal gear serviceable, maintaining effective camouflage, not crapping in the only source of clean water—but they are essential for every member of a unit to accomplish if the unit is to accomplish *its* mission.

Just as there are continuing actions for every phase of a military operation, there are continuing actions for coming home. These are individual actions, personal in nature and easy to avoid doing—especially because nobody has ever defined them as part of a warrior's duty. But they are part of our duty and we cannot outsource them to anybody else. Nobody can stand this watch for us.

There's no hand-holding here, no discussions of inner-children or re-aligning of chakras. This book offers a pragmatic approach to the personal actions each of us must take in the final phase of the warrior's journey. We cannot even begin this phase, however, if we remain on the surface level of supposed glory, banter, and bravado. Those shields served us well in combat but now it's time to set them aside. To move into the final phase requires the bravery to stop hiding from our own human emotions and the courage to descend into the depths of our hearts and minds.

This is nothing we've ever been trained to do, so there are some basic considerations to address before charging ahead. This book will explore the challenges common to warriors after combat, suggest tactics and techniques for how to overcome them, and identify supporting arms available. It's your battle to fight; these are your demons to take on and your lessons to learn. But you don't have to go into it blind and alone. Let this book help and guide you.

You've accepted the challenge to serve and have done your duty in dangerous and difficult situations. But you're not done yet. Take a knee and drink water—because now it's time to begin the next, and final, phase of the warrior's journey.

PART ONE:

THE WARRIOR'S JOURNEY—

WHAT WE DON'T KNOW

1

NONE OF THIS IS NEW

A FEW YEARS BEFORE the invasion of Iraq, Mongo (his mom didn't name him that; we—his friends—did) was flying a Cobra helicopter with a senior officer from our squadron. Crossing a huge desert training range, they heard the electronic beeping of an Emergency Locator Transmitter (ELT) coming through their radios. Knowing a stricken aircraft must be nearby, they began searching and soon spotted smoke rising above the desert scrub. Not far away from the blackened remains of the jet, they saw the pilot, still strapped in his ejection seat and not moving. After landing the Cobra beside the wreckage, the senior officer sent Mongo over to verify the pilot was dead. His undeployed parachute left no question, but they still had to confirm it.

After visually examining the burnt body, Mongo got back in the Cobra expecting the training mission was over and that they would return to base. After all, they'd just found a dead pilot—there must be some paperwork they had to do. But the senior officer had no intention of going home. Acting as if nothing had happened, he ordered Mongo to continue the flight while he radioed their findings at the crash site to Range Control.

Mongo did a pretty good job of pushing the dead pilot out of his mind, but his basic air-work and instrument approaches for the rest of the flight were sub-par. When they finally returned to base, the senior officer was savage in his debrief of Mongo's instrument-flying skills and publicly demanded he be scheduled for remedial training. The rest of the young pilots in the squadron commiserated with Mongo but understood the point: We were expected to focus on our mission, nothing else.

That particular senior officer was a flaming asshole, but his point was valid and in keeping with the general attitude among most people in dangerous professions: To allow tragedy to distract us is dangerous and unacceptable. There's just no room for distracting emotions when death is always milliseconds away.

Controlling these emotions keeps us alive, focused, and fighting for the men and women counting on us to accomplish our mission. This is a good thing—in some cases the most important thing—but it comes at a cost.

THE COMBAT MINDSET

The mindset that subordinates or shuts off emotion is common among warriors. Our ethos demands strength in the face of all adversity, and any perceived weakness is ruthlessly rooted out and destroyed. I learned early in my career that strength meant remaining firmly focused on the external threats and challenges of flying a helicopter gunship—regardless of what was happening around me. That single-minded focus served me well when, in spring 2003, I flew across the border into Iraq.

I was at the peak of my game. A Marine captain with over 1200 flight hours in the AH-1W SuperCobra, I knew my aircraft inside and out and was brimming with confidence. I wasn't afraid of getting killed or wounded; my main worry was that the war might not happen at all. When it finally did, I felt a sense of relief.

My confidence was appropriately placed. I'd been on active duty for over seven years by the time we invaded. Every physical challenge I would face in Iraq had been thoroughly addressed by years of realistic training—on the ground, in the air, and while deployed overseas. That training allowed me to handle surface-level threats effectively to the point where destroying Iraqi soldiers took very little conscious effort on my part. Behind those physical challenges, though, behind the mechanical manipulation of controls and switches and the application of tactics and weapons, inner conflicts were brewing. Being technically and tactically proficient did nothing to protect me from the realization that my actions were violating the basic tenets of humanity. War, and its inherent cheapening of life, poses deeply personal challenges to any normal human and I was no exception. But these internal challenges had never been mentioned in my training, so I thought myself weak when they began to intrude into my life.

Restlessness, an inability to relax when there was nothing pressing to do, and a craving for more action made me uneasy and irritable during lulls in the fighting. Something told me that quiet reflection was very dangerous, and I shunned profound thoughts of any type.

While engaged in combat, the unease was suppressed—physical battles had priority and I was not about to make the enemy's job easier by allowing myself to get distracted. But when I came home, it was a different story. At home I had no external threats to worry about, no physical battles to throw myself into. Without those distractions, the effects of my neglected inner challenges became harder, and eventually impossible, to ignore.

I wrote about my experiences in Iraq, and how they followed me home, in *After Action: The True Story of a Cobra Pilot's Journey*. I will not rehash that story here and only mention it in case you want more information about where I'm coming from with this whole "warrior" thing.[4] In that first book, I exposed all

---

[4] In my experience, most of the people who spout-off about "warriors" have either never met one or have an agenda. Feel free to check out my bona fides and decide for yourself where I fall on that spectrum.

the internal second-guessing I'd gone through during my first tour and how I avoided dealing with the aftermath by drinking and redeploying the first chance I got. I really had no idea how *After Action* would be received and was nervous about how other warriors would react to it. I imagined conversations between Marines I'd served with that dissolved in derisive laughter at the mere mention of my name.

"I never would have figured Shoe to be a pussy. . . . Who knew he was such a weakling? . . . Guess he just wasn't strong enough to handle it."

But, instead of contempt, the responses I got from veterans of all services and conflicts were overwhelmingly supportive. I'd hit on something universal we'd all experienced but refused to mention because we thought we were the only one. Marines, sailors, soldiers, airmen, police officers, paramedics—it didn't matter. None of us had received training for how to deal with the emotions generated by what we'd been called to do. Even the legitimacy of our basic human reactions was denied because our training hadn't deemed them important enough to even mention. There was just no appropriate way to express those emotions without violating our warrior personas. So we hid them—and began suffering the consequences.

WE'RE NOT ALONE

Since I wrote *After Action*, many veterans have told me their own personal struggles after coming home from combat. World War II, Vietnam, Liberia . . . the particular conflict is irrelevant. They all left indelible marks on the men and women who fought in them. Some marks were made apparent by external reactions while others eroded the veteran from within. These injuries came in the form of psychological wounds variously called shell shock, battle fatigue, soldier's heart, or most recently, Post Traumatic Stress Disorder (PTSD). But sometimes they took a different, less clearly defined form. Veterans spoke about feeling disconnected from themselves, alienated from the person they were before combat. It wasn't on the surface—they could resurrect the shell of who they were and fool just about anybody if they wanted to— but deep down they didn't know who they were anymore. Others described their postcombat lives as "hollow" and expressed a certain jealousy of their buddies who'd died in combat—at least they'd gone out on top. Regardless of the specifics of the veterans' experiences, their lives were split into "before" and "after." And the reality of the "after" phase was not something they were prepared for.

Just like past wars, the veterans of Iraq and Afghanistan are coming home with invisible wounds. That this most recent generation of veterans is experiencing the same postcombat challenges as their predecessors is proof, not only that these reactions are normal, but also that we haven't learned how to handle them.

TREASURES FROM THE PAST

Has anybody ever had a good understanding of these challenges? The answer is yes, but we seem to have forgotten it—and where to find it.

Joseph Campbell was a comparative mythologist who studied the cultural mythology of civilizations and societies throughout history. His work and insights are widely respected because he explained how myths contain truths about universal human experiences and provide roadmaps through many of life's challenges. One of his greatest contributions came from his examination of the heroic monomyth, an archetypal human journey reflected in the hero myths of disparate cultures around the globe.

Campbell discovered that tales of great heroes contained the same general sequence and components whether they came from ancient Greece or an Inuit tribe in the frigid north. The path is this: The hero separates from the known world, overcomes a series of trials to gain something of value, and then returns to the known world to share that valuable treasure with his people.

On the surface it looks simple, but this path, recorded over thousands of years by civilizations large and small, exposes a critical gap in our modern warrior's journey: We have forgotten how to return.

The heroes Campbell studied were of myth and legend, not flesh and blood. But when I read his work, I saw how I, and millions of other veterans, had closely followed the initial stages of the journey he described. More importantly, I saw how the absence of guidance for the final stage of this journey forces modern warriors to recreate ancient knowledge on their own—or suffer the consequences.

A MINOR ROADBLOCK

Campbell's research illuminated a pathway through the challenges many modern veterans face, but he unknowingly denied us access by labeling it "The Hero's Journey." This is because "hero" is a loaded word for veterans. But when you take into account how its meaning has changed over time, you can understand why "hero" so accurately describes these ancient warriors—and ourselves.

In ancient Greece, a hero was not a godlike personage devoid of human frailties. In fact, a person bearing that label was as likely to be feared as to be loved. It is this type of hero, rather than a John Wayne character, that Campbell was referring to.

Ancient Greek heroes were men of pain who were both needed by their people and *dangerous* to them. Achilles' withdrawal resulted in numberless Greek deaths; Odysseus' long return home to Ithaca caused more than seven hundred Ithacan deaths on the way or when he got there. Achilles harmed the Greek army during the war; Odysseus harmed his people after the war. They were both heroes in the ancient Greek sense. (Jonathan Shay, *Odysseus in America*, p.2)

While many of our actions clearly fit the template established by these ancient heroes, being called a hero still makes many, if not most, veterans uncomfortable. And I don't think pointing out the shifting linguistic meaning of the word is going to change that. While the general population considers it an appropriate moniker for everybody in uniform, veterans have a much higher standard that must be met before they'll bestow that label on anyone. Even Dakota Meyers, winner of the Medal of Honor in Afghanistan, refused to accept the label of hero.

When the president hung that medal around my neck, I felt glum. I couldn't smile and I said nothing. I gave no remarks and avoided the press. As a Marine, you either bring your team home alive or you die trying. My country was recognizing me for being a failure and for the worst day of my life. (Dakota Meyers and Bing West, *Into the Fire*, p.160)

Regardless of how the interpretation of the word has changed over time, none of us is likely to self-identify as a hero. This is because we've seen our heroes in action. We've lived with them, fought alongside them, and—more often than not—buried them. And I've never once met a hero who considers himself one.

But we can identify with Campbell's "Hero's Journey" with one small adjustment—by substituting "warrior" for "hero." For me, this substitution sidestepped the whole issue and brought Campbell's work out of the abstract and into my own, personal, reality. By calling it the "warrior's journey," I could see how my experiences fit into the archetypal path that Campbell identified without feeling like I was making myself or my experiences out to be more than they were. That small shift gave me a valuable new way to view the entirety of my journey into, and eventually out of, Iraq.

WHAT WE'RE NOT PREPARED FOR

The challenges of initiation into the military, and subsequent years of specialized training, prepared me extremely well for the external challenges I faced in Iraq. But they neglected to address the internal challenges that are inevitable in combat. It was almost as though the institution of the military decided to "wish" the internal ones out of existence by acting like they weren't there. This program worked as intended and set me up for success in combat. Afterward, I continued to follow the assumptions of my training and believed the physical act of returning home signaled that my journey was over—even though a strong sense of unfinished business told me it wasn't.

When I first got home, I viewed my difficulties adjusting to life after combat as black marks on my otherwise respectable record of warrior-ness. I thought the very existence of them made me a poser, a fake, not a real warrior. Who gets overcome by emotions and reactions long after the fact? I viewed those events in my life as history, things I was lucky to have lived through and glad to have in my rearview mirror. That I couldn't seem to get past them called into question my right to call myself a warrior. But when I read Campbell's work, I saw it differently. The adjustment challenges I was struggling with were not taking place after my warrior's journey was complete—they were *part* of the journey—*they are part of the journey*. They were the second, inner, set of trials I had to face.

Understanding that the challenges a warrior must overcome are not limited to the physical put my postcombat life in perspective. This perspective showed me that I had more obstacles to overcome, more battles to fight before I could even *begin* the "return" phase. Just having survived my experiences was not enough—I had to wrest some knowledge, something of value, from them. Only then could I complete my return by sharing it with others.

For the modern military institution, the fundamental components of the ancient warrior's journey have been lost somewhere in time, buried beneath technological advancements that make spiritual concepts seem antiquated. Like an archaeologist, Campbell dug up these components and saw value in them from a scholar's standpoint. But their value is not limited to academic discussions. The steps that make up the ancient warrior's journey highlight what is missing from our own journeys as modern warriors.

The modern warrior's journey provides a clear path for the warrior to follow into combat—but then it ends. There is no guidance or direction given for how to come back. It's almost like the creators of our version didn't know how to come home themselves, so the path they laid out for us just stopped. This leads us to believe our journey as warriors should end when we physically return home—and inserts denial at the head of an already long list of challenges we must overcome.

The ancient version of the warrior's journey is far more comprehensive. It offers a path that not only leads the warrior *into* challenges and adventures, but also *out* of them. When taken in its entirety, the ancient warrior's journey is a circle. It never really ends, and the valuable treasures gained through adventure are constantly being reinvested by the warrior's return.

We may not have been trained to complete the warrior's journey, but, if we take the time to examine how the universal human experiences Campbell identified in mythology apply to our own lives, we can figure out how to do it on our own.

INTERNAL BATTLES—WHAT'S THE BIG DEAL?

What's the big deal? Why do I have to do anything else other than survive and come home? Isn't that enough?

Apparently not.

It doesn't take a particularly astute observer to notice that veterans experience more than their fair share of problems in our society. Are they all based in combat experiences? No, of course not. But there are enough of us who have gone to war and been changed by our experiences in fundamental ways to show that something is obviously going on. It means that the status quo—how we've always done things—isn't working. If we want to improve how veterans re-integrate after combat, then we have to break out of the inaccurate and dangerous assumption that our battles are only external in nature. We must recognize that the inner battles are real—and also choose to face them.

This is a difficult decision to make for several reasons, chief among them is the fact that many of us don't know the choice even exists, let alone that making it is integral to, not a betrayal of, a warrior's identity. Instead of choosing to face these inner challenges, most of us ignore their presence and turn away. This forces us to remain on the surface level of emotions and reactions because we can't trust what might come out if we go deeper. We suppress the unease and make excuses to ourselves when it infiltrates our daily lives. We feel that nobody who wasn't with us in combat could possibly understand so we clam up, preferring to lock painful experiences away rather than suffer the blank stares of incomprehension. One or two drinks help us relax and have fun—but any more than that and we retreat into ourselves, emerging only when unexpected anger prompts us to lash out.

This is the result of stagnating along the warrior's journey, and it is dangerously easy to do. We can stop progressing at any time—all we have to do is refuse to face the challenges that come our way. When we avoid the challenges, when we suppress the reactions and emotions of the past instead of dealing with them head on, then we stop moving forward on our journey. This stagnation can last a minute or a lifetime, and, unless we're really lucky, nobody will ever poke us in the chest and tell us to get moving. We can stay there, held hostage by past events and emotions, for as long as we want. As long as we do, though, we'll be living half-lives—lives devoid of emotional interactions at meaningful levels, wrought with failed relationships and missed opportunities.

What if you got back a long time ago and have been stationary since? Have you missed your opportunity to successfully return home? Absolutely not. It doesn't matter how long you've stagnated—minutes or decades—the road ahead remains open to you. To begin moving again requires nothing more than the qualities that you have already demonstrated—courage, dedication, and willingness to do what must be done. These warrior traits reside within you now just as they did when you chose to serve. They provided the fortitude that sustained you through the trials of initiation into the military and the external challenges of combat. Now they can help you overcome the inner battles that stand between you and the rest of your life.

What if you're still on active duty? What if your external battles are not complete yet? If that's your situation, then you're lucky. You have the opportunity to expand your understanding of the universal warrior experience in real time—as you go through it. This does not mean that you drop the mental protection of compartmentalization and attempt to absorb everything that comes your way. But reading this book and recognizing the normalcy of your own reactions and emotions will equip you for a smoother return from combat—when that time comes. When it does, the knowledge you've gained will help you locate your position along the warrior's journey and enhance your ability to understand and overcome the particular challenges you face.

RETREAT, HELL.

Stagnate or move ahead, there is no other option. Regardless of how long you've served or how long ago you came home, one thing is certain: You'll never revert to the person you were before you started. Good thing, too, because that's not the goal of the journey. The goal is to complete the transformation that began the day you chose to serve. What lies at the end of this transformation? A wiser, more self-aware veteran who has descended into the depths of the unknown and returned with knowledge to share.

How to share it? That's up to you.

Maybe you will continue in public service, bringing the hard-earned lessons of your experiences into the government. Or maybe you'll be the high school teacher who reaches that one student nobody else could, or the coach who injects deeper concepts of sportsmanship and duty into their team. Or maybe you'll just be the person who gets the phone call at 0200 from a drunk buddy from the war who's at the end of his rope. What you say to the muffled sobs at the end of the line could make the difference between life or death.

Regardless of how you choose to share your knowledge, the transformation you complete by facing the inner challenges of the warrior's journey will provide a solid foundation for the rest of your life. The experiences of the past will still be there but they won't interrupt anymore. They'll take their rightful place as defining moments in your past and will stop injecting raw emotions into your present. You'll move forward in life bearing the confidence of your experiences and a maturity others will recognize and respect—even if they don't understand why.

But there are significant obstacles to overcome first. Our modern military training does not include returning home as something a warrior must prepare for. This leads to perceptions of weakness, of being "the only one" having difficulties adjusting, and reinforces a one-dimensional concept of what it means to be a warrior that has kept many veterans from ever fully coming home. We reinforce these obstacles in our own minds by viewing ourselves through a lens fogged by other's perceptions. But if we examine the reality of our situation as it relates to the experiences of warriors past, the lens becomes clear.

The next chapter is devoted to exactly that—wiping the lens clean.

2

DEADLY
MISCONCEPTIONS

MECHANICAL ADJUSTMENTS are easy. If a pistol-shooter consistently hits low on the target, it's more than likely they're anticipating the shot. A good pistol coach can break that bad habit and have them drilling the bull's-eye in short order. The same cannot be said for mental adjustments.

Mental adjustments cannot be externally imposed—they have to come from within. In order for us to change how we perceive the world, we need some motivation, some personal understanding of why the adjustment is necessary. Years of inertia must be overcome before most people will even listen to a different viewpoint, let alone change theirs. This is certainly the case when it comes to veterans' expectations of how they *should* be able to return from combat. Based in wishful thinking, these comforting fairy tales encourage stagnation and are among the first of the obstacles veterans must face when they come home. They were for me.

Like many veterans, I figured that I should be able to just move on after I came home from Iraq. When it became obvious that I couldn't, my first reaction wasn't to ask for help. I didn't look inward for clues to what was bothering me or even consider trying to figure out how my experiences had impacted me. No, my first reaction was denial.

This isn't happening to me. No way, not this guy.

My reaction was not unique. As Americans, we're bombarded by examples of fictional heroes "strong enough" to remain unaffected by the carnage and mayhem around them. Consciously or not, these images shape our expectations that we, as real warriors, should be strong enough to be unaffected as well. But after we get home, and the evidence mounts that something actually *is* bothering us, we feel betrayed by some personal shortcoming we never knew existed. Because our misconceptions tell us those reactions are symptoms of weakness, we put all our efforts into hiding them—and stagnate on our journey as a result.

The assumptions I'd made—well before actually going to war—about how I should be able to come home gave me only one choice: Ignore the pain and unease or admit to being a weakling. There was no other option. My misconceptions told me I should be able to move on with my life like previous generations, that my experiences were nowhere near as traumatic as other veterans', and that nothing I'd been through rated feeling the slightest unease. It was only after examining these misconceptions that I saw how they'd trapped me—and continue to trap millions of others.

FINDING THE POO[5]

Challenging these misconceptions is an obstacle that keeps many of us from ever moving forward after combat. Instead, we build walls of denial that keep even the bravest from ever leaving the safety of our mental Forward Operating Bases (FOBs). Barricaded behind HESCOs[6] filled with assumptions and hearsay, men and women who've demonstrated tremendous courage in the past meekly accept indirect fire attacks as thoughts of "I'm a puss,"

---

[5] POO stands for Point Of Origin, a term used to describe the originating location of indirect fire.

[6] HESCO barriers are basically open-top, industrial-size sandbags used to make walls to protect FOBs from direct and indirect fire.

"I should be strong enough to ignore this," and "What's wrong with me?" impact all around them. Although they have the power to do so, they never go outside the wire to hunt down and kill the misconceptions launching these thoughts. Instead, they accept the limitations of life under a state of perpetual siege.

A series of events in my own life—my brother's near fatal helicopter crash, the responsibilities of fatherhood, and my wife's refusal to allow me to stagnate—prompted me to abandon the walls of denial that had formed my FOB. I might have dug in even deeper, though, built my walls higher and hidden behind thicker barriers, if it hadn't been for the confusion those events generated within me. My overreaction to the news of my brother's crash, fear of passing my burdens on to my children, and the widening gap between my wife and me forced me to make a decision— barricade forever or take action. It somehow felt cowardly to sit behind a barricade, so, five years after coming home, I decided to get off my ass. The mission that followed hasn't been easy, but it's been worth it. By leaving the supposed safety of denial, I was finally able to locate, close with, and destroy the misconceptions that had been making me feel like a weakling.

These misconceptions are common among veterans, so dragging them into the open and examining them is a worthwhile exercise. To start with, let's take a closer look at why, with a stack of medals on my chest and two combat tours under my belt, I believed my right to call myself a warrior was so tenuous that it could be erased if I admitted feeling any aftereffects from what I'd been through.

THE GREATEST GENERATION

It is historically typical for returning American war veterans throughout our history to be ignored

> by the communities they returned to, rather than
> to be celebrated and cherished by them. The expe-
> rience of the World War II veterans—the fathers of
> the Vietnam veterans—is the historical *anomaly*.
> —Jonathan Shay, *Odysseus in America* p.154

Of all the conflicts in our nation's history, the one I figured
least likely to cause lasting aftereffects among our veterans was
World War II (WWII). Wasn't that the "good war?" Weren't the
lines of good and evil clearly drawn and obvious? Didn't the
entire nation mobilize for the common good of the world? And
after the ticker-tape stopped falling, didn't everyone buy a new
Chevy, impregnate his wife, go to college, and build postwar
America into a superpower? From everything I'd absorbed from
movies and books about the veterans of WWII, it seemed like,
while some had suffered horrible wounds, they returned generally healthy, emotionally whole, and moved onward in their lives
without a hitch. This rosy view of the WWII veteran experience
formed my expectations of what I, with my relatively short dura-
tions of combat in Iraq, should be able to do when I got home.
If those guys could endure the horrors of Guadalcanal and Iwo
Jima and be fine, then I sure as hell should be able to do the same
after An Nasiriyah. They set the bar high but I figured I was
tough enough to reach it.

Then I read Thomas Childers' *Soldier from the War
Returning* and realized my perceptions were based in fantasy,
selective memory, and Hollywood fairy dust. In his prologue, the
University of Pennsylvania history professor attacks the "blanket
of nostalgic adulation" Americans have used to "muffle . . . the
complex, often painful realities of their postwar experiences
. . . the most prominent expression of which is found in Tom
Brokaw's best-selling book *The Greatest Generation*."

This glowing homage has become more than a tribute to a passing generation; it has become our public memory of the war and its aftermath, a quasi-official transcript of events that glides sentimentally over what for many veterans was a deeply troubled reentry into a civilian world that, like themselves, had undergone dramatic change. (Childers, p.4)

And what characterized the "deeply troubled reentry" Childers mentions?

. . . unemployment among veterans was rampant— triple that of civilians in 1947. Housing was also hard to find. . . . In early 1946, an estimated 1.5 million veterans were living with friends or family, and in some cities as many as one-third of all married veterans were living with a friend or relative. (Childers, p.7)

And those were just the material challenges of coming home. What about the psychological ones? Again, my rose-colored glasses had given me the false impression that the noble aspects of WWII had protected its veterans from postcombat adjustment challenges.

Post-traumatic stress disorder was not diagnosed until 1980, but in the aftermath of the Second World War, depression, recurring nightmares, survivor guilt, outbursts of rage (most frequently directed at family members), "exaggerated startle responses," and anxiety reactions—all of which are recognized today as classic symptoms of PTSD—were as common as they were unnerving. (Childers, p.8)

Professor Childers rounded out my education when he tied the unaddressed emotional aftereffects of WWII veterans to those suffered by veterans of other wars:

> It is time to confront the emotional aftershocks of the Second World War, not just for aging veterans, many of whom are turning up in VA hospitals with undiagnosed chronic or delayed-onset PTSD, but also for a new generation of men and women struggling to adjust to a life interrupted and forever changed by war. . . .

> Long consigned to a dim corner of our public memory, many of the same deeply disturbing social and personal problems arising from the wars in Vietnam, Iraq, and Afghanistan were glaringly present in the aftermath of the Second World War. (Childers, p.13)

The veterans of World War II did fight bravely amid terrible circumstances. And they also helped America become the strongest nation on earth after they came home. But they did not do it without inner torment, ruined marriages, and incredible personal burdens that became family legacies of pain. They hid their pain because that's what they were expected to do—and lived forever in its clutches.

COMPARING APPLES TO ORANGES

The second misconception I faced stemmed from my habit of measuring my experiences against other people's. I imagined the experiences of combat spread along a static gradation of trauma. On one end might be stubbing your toe, and on the other, the Bataan Death March. Because I never examined it closely, this assumption imposed an artificial measurement of the relative trauma I felt I *should* have experienced based on where my experiences fell on the spectrum. I hadn't stormed the beach in Normandy, hadn't slithered through tunnels in Cu Chi, or held a friend's head as he died. My experiences were somewhere above a stubbed toe but certainly not bad enough to rate aftereffects.

Yet there they were.

And the fact that I couldn't just ignore the aftereffects, couldn't just suppress the unease and make it go away, called into question my own fortitude. If other veterans have been through much tougher situations and seem fine, then what the hell is wrong with me? Renowned psychiatrist Jonathan Shay describes this reaction as creating "hierarchies of suffering" and labels it one of the major impediments to healing that combat veterans impose on themselves. This common misconception, based in making comparisons, is hard to ignore because the supposed evidence is right there—he served three tours while I only served two; she got shot and I never did; he patrolled Lashkar Gah while I just flew over Baghdad . . .

A former squadron mate of my father unwittingly (?) reinforced this misconception in his review of my book, *After Action,* on Amazon. In it he stated, "The author dealt with many issues we former veterans didn't seem to like to talk about, but I was very taken aback by how affected these young men were following only a few weeks of combat." This Vietnam veteran seems to have assumed, like I used to, that you could apply objective metrics like time and intensity of events to an experience like combat and come up with a threshold that would determine aftereffects—below it you're fine, above it you're a mess. There's a fair amount of bravado mixed in here as well, a feeling that

"We had it much tougher and turned out fine—what's wrong with you?" that gave his comment added sting.

But you can't measure the impact of experiences like that. Does it matter if a person is exposed to one second or ten years in combat? Not to that person. What matters is the impact that person's experiences had on them—and that cannot be measured solely by duration or even by their intense or dramatic nature. What I experience inwardly in a given situation can be very different from the impact that same event has on you, the person standing next to me. My personal experience and yours are *that* unique.

The urge to downplay our own experiences is deeply ingrained in our warrior ethos. We all know men and women who've done incredible things yet remain humble about their accomplishments. This humbleness enhances their status in our eyes and is an attribute that is worthy of emulation. But it is not humility that inhibits us from honestly examining how our experiences have affected us. It is fear.

We fear that some imaginary council of ultimate warriors will apply the same false calculus to our experiences and decide, once and for all, that we are weak. We fear that our comrades will somehow think less of us, that our right to call ourselves warriors will be revoked, or that we'll forfeit the respect we would have enjoyed if we'd just been strong enough to keep telling ourselves that others had it tougher and are fine.

I hope I've made this misconception sound childish because, well, it is. That doesn't mean it will be easy to overcome, though. Just remember, when it comes to determining what events hold the power to destroy your life long after they're over, only your internal experiences matter. Fear of what somebody else might, or might not, think? C'mon, we left junior high school a long time ago.

A SKILL HALF-TAUGHT

The third misconception I had to overcome was the most insidious. It stemmed from the very efficiency of the training I had received and highlights a primary shortcoming in how we perceive the challenges of being a warrior.

Long before I ever imagined I would become a pilot, flying was a part of my life. My father was a Navy pilot, like his father before him, and my early memories are studded with old airplanes, air shows, and airports. Seizing an opportunity to educate my brother and sister and me, Dad named our first four or five parakeets "Bernoulli" after the Swiss mathematician who explained how a wing creates lift. It was years before I stopped trying to look under the wings of passing planes to see the little brightly colored birds pushing it up in the sky.

I was slightly less clueless when I reported to flight school as a Marine Second Lieutenant years later, but it didn't matter. The instructors assumed I had never seen an aircraft and started from the ground up. The training covered every possible contingency and was so thorough I'm convinced they could have taught a monkey how to fly.

This same scenario was repeated multiple times throughout my military training. Instructors always assumed I knew nothing, and every challenge I was expected to encounter was identified and clearly explained to me. Only after I understood every aspect of the challenge was I given concrete instructions for overcoming it. And I wasn't trained to deal only with physical challenges, but with mental ones as well.

But the preparation I received for the mental challenges of combat did not follow the normal template of military training. Instead of exhaustively explaining these challenges and then dictating thorough steps to overcome them, this training was informal and hodgepodge. In fact, the entirety of my preparation for the mental challenges of combat consisted of honing just one skill—compartmentalization.

I was expected to take anything that could potentially distract me and ignore it. A fender-bender on the way to work? Stuff it away before climbing in the cockpit. Break up with, or knock up, my girlfriend? Don't think about it while flying. Bullets cracking past the cockpit or a buddy's bird crashing in flames? Drive on and accomplish the mission. From the mundane to the extreme, I was taught that emotions and reactions were dangerous distractors that could get me or my comrades killed—or worse, fail to complete our mission.

Compartmentalization was my mental flak jacket. It protected me from emotional reactions and allowed my other training to guide me through the physical challenges that were generating them. Focus on the mission, stuff anything uncomfortable or painful away, and drive on. As essential as this was for survival in combat, there was something vital missing from what I'd been taught of compartmentalization.

You can't do it forever.

You see, compartmentalization is a short-term solution— kind of like a tourniquet. When applied during an emergency, there is a good chance it will save your life. But nobody walks around with a tourniquet for any longer than it takes to get to a hospital. It hurts, you can't use the appendage, and there's a good chance that it is destroying parts of you while saving your life. No, you get to medical attention and they remove the tourniquet as soon as safely possible.

James Wright, author of *Those Who Have Borne the Battle*, highlights the destructive effects of keeping this mental tourniquet on too long. In this book, he quotes Bobby Muller, a paralyzed Vietnam veteran and organizer of Vietnam Veterans of America, in 1979:

> . . . Muller told a reporter that while going to war was traditionally a defining experience in anyone's life, Vietnam veterans had learned to keep quiet about it. He said that "we came home and were told we were either fools or killers. Guys came home after this significant life experience and they've never had the opportunity to talk about it. It's torn people apart. It's unnatural." (Wright, p.207)

Somehow this lesson never made it into my instructors' training manuals. The requirement to take the mental tourniquet off—to de-compartmentalize—was never even hinted at in any of my training. It was simply never discussed, like it didn't exist. So when my unease followed me home from Iraq, when caustic emotions from my past started to seep into my present, I was worse than unprepared. My "go-to" move, what I'd been taught and had used effectively in the past, turned out to be exactly the *wrong* thing to do.

Without recognizing the dangers, I doubled down on compartmentalization. I ignored the signs that something was bothering me, that I was reacting differently and was uncomfortable in my own skin. I assumed these were symptoms of some latent weakness that was just now, after two combat tours, making itself known. I didn't recognize them as unavoidable reactions to continued compartmentalization, and it didn't even cross my mind to take that tourniquet off. Instead, I redoubled my efforts to hide the unease, to bury it away like I had in combat. Angrily, I berated myself for being so weak as to let it show at all.

This is the misconception that is the hardest to overcome. We trust that our training thoroughly prepared us for every challenge we were expected to encounter. Why? Because for the most part it did. So if we encounter a challenge we weren't prepared for, we don't assume it was overlooked. Rather, we assume the fault lies with us, that we should be able to overcome it with what we *had* been taught.

As a result, most of us just try to stuff the memories and emotions of combat away when we come home. Then, when they inject rage, terror, guilt, and fear into our daily lives, we get mad at ourselves for failing to keep them under wraps before stuffing them away again. But this just reprimes the pump and ensures the suppressed emotions will escape again later on. By teaching only one skill, one defense mechanism against the mental rigors of being a warrior, our training set us up for success in combat but failure at home.

These failures don't have to be extreme. You don't have to snort your paycheck up your nose for months on end, ride your motorcycle at 120mph on the highway, or fight everybody who looks crossways at you to fail at coming home. Those sorts of catastrophes make for compelling stories, but they are not indicative of most veterans' experiences. Most veterans come home and put genuine effort into moving forward in life, focusing on their family, and being productive members of society. Does it matter if his children don't know him very well? Or if she buries herself in work because it's the only time she doesn't have to be reminded of the past? Why should we be concerned when our families excuse our behavior with an embarrassed, "We don't know—he was just never the same after the war"? Or stop having beer or wine in the house when we come to visit because our mood swings are too unpredictable after a few drinks? These, and many other indicators that we have not come to grips with our experiences, erode us quietly from within. They may not be dramatic failures worthy of the evening news, but they can screw up our lives nonetheless.

IN THE ABSENCE OF ORDERS . . .

We have come a long way from the days when knights provided their own weapons and horses when they went to fight. Today, a compact exists between the citizen who volunteers to serve and the nation that benefits from their service: We'll provide the training and tools, you provide the blood, sweat, courage, and commitment to get the job done. And Americans have gotten the job done over and over again. But, as we've discovered, just getting the job done overseas is not the end of the warrior's journey. There is a long road to be traveled afterward that is not covered by a modern warrior's training. This training is sufficient to get us *into* combat and emerge victorious, but not to return home.

There's no conspiracy here, no dark force bent on creating a class of warriors capable of fighting and nothing else. The reason modern warriors are not prepared for the challenges of coming home is simple: These are individual challenges, and the means to overcome them will vary with each individual. Military training is not known for enhancing individuality, or the skills required for introspection, and those who exhibit those traits while in the military are "encouraged" to hide them. Over time, they wither away from disuse. Ironically, those are the very traits and skills a warrior needs in order to process, learn, and grow from his experiences.

To continue progressing along the warrior's journey, a modern warrior has to move past the belt-fed, Ooh-Rah, yut-yut mentality of just following orders—because eventually there are no orders. Outside the military there is nobody providing clear guidance for what to do and how to do it. No external power can impose measures designed to usher you into the final stage of the warrior's journey. You have to do it yourself. You have to become your own pistol coach, identify where your rounds are hitting, and then figure out what adjustments to make to get them into the black.

The first thing you'll have to do is seize the initiative. In the absence of orders, you have to *choose* to face the challenges before you, *choose* to patrol outside your wire, and *choose* to challenge the assumptions holding you hostage. But you can't just start firing from the hip—you need to have a plan.

Nobody likes mission planning. It's a pain in the ass and gets in the way of all the fun stuff like working out, shooting, and jumping out of planes. But it's essential if the mission is to be a success.

The next three chapters might feel like mission planning, but rest assured, they're essential if you are to overcome the challenges ahead. So, eat your spinach, take your vitamins, do your PME[7]—all the crap we don't want to do but must in order to be ready for the trials to come—and keep reading.

Don't worry. Eventually you get to jump out of the plane.

---

[7] Professional Military Education: Formal academic coursework required before a service member can be promoted to a higher rank.

3

THE MYTHIC POWER
OF WAR

War is a mythic arena. In its noise and grandiosity, its manipulation of the forces of life and death, and its irrevocable shaping of history and destiny, war transforms the mundane into the epic and legendary.

—Edward Tick, *War and the Soul*, p.25

WAR HAS BEEN HELD as a rite of passage for thousands of years. Traditionally, it was the crucible boys had to survive in order to become men. Even now, many veterans consider it the dividing line between their own adolescence and adulthood. But even if we value the experiences of war in this fashion, few of us understand why. It's not as if the soldiers on D-Day were considering "the shaping of history and destiny" as they waited for their landing-craft ramp to drop. Nor were Marines mulling over the "manipulation of the forces of life and death" while patrolling Sadr City. And how many of us felt particularly "epic and legendary" scooping our comrades into body-bags?

Not many. But that's not to say the statement by Tick is incorrect. In fact, according to men and women who've faced combat, as well as those who help them address the challenges of coming home, he's right on. The experiences of war rate such mystical, grandiose descriptions because they transform those who survive them—often without their knowledge or permission. Even if we refuse to admit it or just don't see it, the man or woman who emerges from the "mythic arena" of war is not the same as the one who entered.

This is because we're human, and our battles take place on two levels—outer and inner. The outer battles are the physical ones, the application of explosives, steel, and lead against flesh. They decide victory or defeat on a grand scale and life or death on a mundane one. Their scope and scale make war epic, monumental, and legendary. But they are not what makes war mythic.

The inner battles do that.

For each action taken in an outer battle, each decision made, tragedy observed, or killing skill applied, there is a corresponding battle that takes place within the warrior. These inner conflicts are what healthy human beings experience when they do, see, or experience things that violate fundamental concepts of humanity. And at a basic level, war violates every aspect of humanity. To even observe modern warfare is to question the existence of anything special or evolved in humans. For those who participate in it, this question is not academic—it's personal. The humanity we question is our own.

Warriors have always had to face these inner battles. The effects of trauma, death, fear, exhilaration, and rage on the human animal have not changed over time. Today's warrior must protect himself against the same emotions and reactions that might have distracted a Roman Centurion thousands of years ago. But the incredible speed, intensity, and lethality of modern warfare mean he accumulates these emotions and reactions at a greater rate than ever before.

As noted in the previous chapter, successful warriors use compartmentalization to protect themselves from being distracted by these inner battles. We have learned to ignore them in the heat of the moment in order to remain focused on the task at hand. This skill is essential for survival in combat, not to mention attaining victory. But while the conscious mind can be shielded from the inner conflicts, the unconscious mind is not so easily protected. It is filming and recording every event. And not only are the sounds, tastes, and smells captured, but all the emotional reactions we ignored in order to survive are registered as well. Stored away, these memories do not dissipate on their own. They exert pressure from deep within and, over time, twist and distort our consciousness like tree roots pushing up a sidewalk.

Exposure to these inner battles changes the way our unconscious mind operates. It weathers the experiences of combat without protection and is forever changed as a result. The conscious mind, however, was protected from those inner battles by the flak jacket of compartmentalization. It continues to operate as though nothing has happened.

And the chasm begins to form.

Instead of a unified voice, the conscious and unconscious minds now speak different languages, at different volumes, and at different times. At a minimum, this rift is annoying. The wider it gets, though, the more destabilizing it becomes. To warriors struggling to ignore its presence, the disconnect between their conscious and unconscious minds strands them between two worlds; they are living in peace but reacting to war.

This was the case for a young Marine I met a few years ago. He'd been an infantry squad leader in Fallujah and Ramadi during the fighting in 2004. A common insurgent tactic during those bloody battles was to arm children—sometimes with real AK-47s, sometimes fake—and send them toward the Marine positions. It was a win-win situation for the insurgents. If the Marines killed the kids, they could claim atrocities. If not, then the kids might actually open fire or get detonated remotely. It was just one more horrible aspect of war that offered no right answer.

One day this young Marine was manning a .50cal on top of a vehicle, covering a foot patrol as it cleared rubbled houses close to their checkpoint. Suddenly, a boy—couldn't have been more than six—burst out of a nearby house, pointing a rifle at him.

Reacting instinctively to the movement, the Marine swung his heavy machine gun to engage. Two facts registered simultaneously in his mind: boy and gun. But within a heartbeat the young father stuffed thoughts of his own son away and focused on his mission. The decision to kill the boy or allow himself and his buddies to die was almost made for him. He might have accepted additional risk to himself, but not for his Marines. He began to depress the butterfly trigger.

At that instant, another Marine burst out of an adjacent doorway and knocked the kid over with a flying tackle. The plastic replica AK-47 went flying as the rolling Marine frantically tried to separate himself from the potentially explosive-laden boy. Time stopped as everybody tensed for the explosion that didn't come. A few moments later the kid scrambled away with bleeding knees and elbows and the patrol moved on, the episode forgotten.

For the Marine with the machine gun, though, the decision to kill a child ripped his conscious and unconscious minds apart. It didn't matter that he hadn't actually killed the boy—he'd decided to. Compartmentalization protected his conscious mind from what he'd almost done, but his unconscious mind registered the full impact of that decision. That incident, seemingly forgotten almost instantly, created a chasm between his conscious and unconscious minds that would have lasting consequences.

He made it home from Iraq in one piece—but then his life began to fall apart. Thoughts of being with his family sustained him during his deployment, yet when he got home he withdrew from them all. He felt uneasy around them and refused to play with his young son or go out with his wife. The only place he felt remotely comfortable was indoors and away from anybody else. His coldness and self-isolation confused and hurt his wife initially, but eventually just became their new normal. He was irritable, quick to flash anger, and could never seem to sit still. He didn't share his experiences in Iraq with anybody, lost touch with the Marines in his squad, and was fundamentally alone.

AFTERMATH

He did receive treatment for PTSD through the Veterans Administration (VA) and even felt minor relief after talking to a counselor there. After multiple sessions, he achieved enough clarity about his situation to engage with his wife and son again, albeit in small doses. Then, after a particularly good day when he was feeling calm and just beginning to believe that things were looking up, it happened.

He was sitting on the couch after playing outside with his son. The TV was on and his wife was in the kitchen making dinner. He wasn't thinking about anything, really, just sitting there, relaxed. Without warning, his son jumped on his back. Little spindly arms grappled around his neck to get a solid hold for a piggy-back ride or mock wrestling session—but he didn't notice. All he knew was that he was being attacked.

Rage, pure molten rage, erupted from the core of his soul. He smashed and thrashed and quickly got a hold of something solid. Ripping the boy off his back, he pushed his little body into the couch and cocked his fist to strike. His wife, alerted by the commotion, screamed.

Her scream brought him back to reality. Shaking, he released his grip and let his arm fall to his side. Then he walked away, stewing in self-loathing and guilt that threatened to overwhelm him. The episode might have been smoothed over, maybe he could have laughed it off like he'd been playing or just told his boy not to sneak up on him again. But he couldn't—he knew he'd been too close. Instead of trying to figure out what happened, he did what so many other veterans have done when war came home with them. He doubled down on compartmentalization and reinforced his mental walls with physical ones. Moving into a cave-like spare bedroom, he withdrew from his family, never coming out if they were around. He just stayed in there alone, isolated, and in pain.

He didn't know why he'd reacted the way he did. He couldn't explain why his startled reaction caused him to hate himself with such ferocity. The only thing he was sure of was that the only way to keep his family safe—from him—was to stay away from them.

THE DARK SIDE OF COMPARTMENTALIZATION

If we went through combat fully conscious of our emotions, we probably wouldn't have to deal with any emotional challenges afterward. Our conscious and unconscious minds would have experienced the same emotions and reactions simultaneously and there would be no chasm to close.

We'd also probably be dead. The distraction of having our conscious mind pummeled by emotional responses would've put our comrades, our mission, and ourselves at risk. So we compartmentalized our reactions, protected our conscious mind, and remained focused on the immediate threats to our survival. Each time we did this, the chasm grew wider.

For many of us, compartmentalization keeps us from even realizing the chasm exists. It is only after we come home that the differences between the person who left and the one who returned become apparent—usually to our family members first. If confronted about this change we may be unable to explain why. All we know is we *are* different now than we were before.

But this phenomenon is not based only in the learned response of compartmentalization. It is also hard-wired into our brains. Pierre Janet, an early pioneer in psychotherapy, was the first to explain how a person can have no recollection of traumatic events yet still be unconsciously influenced by reactions they generated. "Janet noted that post-traumatic amnesia was due to a 'constriction of the field of consciousness' which kept painful memories split off from ordinary awareness." (Judith Lewis Herman, *Trauma and Recovery*, p.45)

Herman builds on Janet's work to explain how a normally functioning brain protects us from these memories:

> Traumatic events produce profound and lasting changes in physiological arousal, emotion, cognition, and memory. Moreover, traumatic events may sever these normally integrated functions from one another. The traumatized person may experience intense emotion but without clear memory of the event, or may remember everything in detail but without emotion. (Herman, p.34)

This split between ordinary awareness and the experiences of war is what lends war a mythic quality. It has this seemingly magical ability to reach in and rewire a person's unconsciousness without their being aware that it's happening. This mythic quality implies incredible transformative power, but it is not inexplicable—or unexpected.

The changes wrought by traumatic experiences have always been part of the warrior's journey. And they are not all bad, either. To a warrior willing to do the hard work to complete their journey, the existence of the chasm offers an opportunity.

Closing the chasm between the conscious and unconscious minds provides the means for the warrior to comprehend his experiences and eventually learn from them. This process breeds wisdom and maturity that is, indeed, mythic. It's just that we, as modern warriors, have not been taught how to close this chasm—or even that it exists.

4

SOCIETY'S ROLE

. . . I cannot escape the suspicion that what we do as mental health professionals is not as good as the healing that in other cultures has been rooted in the native soil of the returning soldier's community.

—Jonathan Shay, *Achilles in Vietnam*, p.194

SOME SOCIETIES THROUGHOUT history had specific ways of helping their warriors heal the inner chasms created by combat trauma. They had rites of passage, rituals, and meaningful ceremonies designed to welcome the returning warrior, cleanse him of the caustic emotions of battle, and reassure him of his honored position within society.

In his book, *No More Heroes*, Richard Gabriel explains the societal support for returning warriors that was commonplace among many, if not all, traditional warrior societies:

> Societies have always recognized that war changes men, that they are not the same after they return. That is why primitive societies often required soldiers to perform purification rites before allowing them to rejoin their communities. These rites often involved washing or other forms of ceremonial cleansing. Psychologically, these rituals provided soldiers with a way of ridding themselves of stress and the terrible guilt that always accompanies the sane after war. It was also a way of treating guilt by providing a mechanism through which fighting men could decompress and relive their terror without feeling weak or exposed. Finally, it was a way of telling the soldier that what he did was right

and that the community for which he fought was grateful and that, above all, his community of sane and normal men welcomed him back. (Gabriel, p.155)

In contrast, the following passage from James Wright—historian, author, and Marine—highlights the general relationship between American society and returning veterans:

Combat veterans then return home. They must suppress their combat experiences in order to return successfully to civil society. But even if they are successfully suppressed, they cannot be forgotten. Each of these tasks of learning and unlearning comes at some cost, and the cost is an intensely personal one that is not borne by society, (Wright, p.16).

Instead of societal support and ritualistic cleansing of guilt, terror, and stress, our veterans have historically been told to just suppress it all and move on. This lack of understanding on the part of society doesn't just ignore the problem of veterans' reintegration, it actively exacerbates it. Instead of facilitating their return, our society unintentionally places additional burdens on returning warriors.

One of these burdens is the sense of isolation many veterans feel after returning home. They've been fundamentally changed by their experiences, even if they don't know how or why, and no longer feel like they fit in. After leaving active duty, veterans in towns and cities across the nation often withdraw from meaningful social interactions with nonveterans to protect themselves from this uncomfortable realization. This response is reinforced by the way our society holds veterans at arm's length—content to idealize but not understand them.

> Too often, this view of the veteran as a man apart
> is shared by civilians, who are content to idealize
> or disparage his military service while avoiding
> detailed knowledge of what that service entailed.
> Social support for the telling of war stories, to the
> extent that it exists at all, is usually segregated
> among combat veterans. . . . Thus the fixation
> of the trauma—the sense of a moment frozen in
> time—may be perpetuated by social customs that
> foster the segregation of warriors from the rest of
> society. (Herman, p.67)

Our society's negative impact on veterans' reintegration is not intentional—I don't think for a minute the American population is unsupportive or insensitive to the issues facing our military. But unreasonable expectations of how veterans "should" be able to return home, and social isolation that denies veterans critical support when they need it most, are real obstacles that derail many veterans' efforts to move on after their service.

This lack of understanding likely stems from the fact that, thankfully, only a small percentage of Americans have ever experienced combat firsthand. This hasn't always been the case but it certainly is now. In the last forty-five years, the percentage of veterans decreased from almost half of the population to less than 7%. In 1969, 45% of the adult male population were veterans.[8] And now, in 2014, there are a little under 22 million American veterans out of a population of 318 million—about 6.8%.[9]

And those are just percentages of the population who've

---

[8] James Wright, *Those Who Have Borne The Battle*, p.228

[9] www.census.gov

worn a uniform—the percentages who've actually engaged in combat are much smaller. There is no reason to expect a society as sheltered from the reality of combat as ours to understand the profound impact it can have on those it sends to fight.

WHAT DOES IT MATTER?

Why should the general population's unfamiliarity with the realities of combat have any impact on returning veterans? Because a society without intimate knowledge of the warrior's outer *and* inner battles cannot provide the support and guidance traditional societies have used to help their warriors reintegrate after war.

Tom Holm's book, *Strong Hearts, Wounded Souls*, brings this concept to light. A Vietnam veteran himself, Holm describes the effects of Native American tribal ceremonies on veterans returning from Vietnam. While the tribes were different, and the ceremonies differed in the details, the rituals and ceremonies were similar in that they were community-based efforts to welcome the warrior home, cleanse him of what he'd had to do in the war, and reintegrate him into the tribe. While the experiences of war were considered impurities that must be cleansed from his soul, the warrior himself was never blamed for those stains. They were simply there and needed to be expunged.

There was an understanding extended to the veteran, an acknowledgement that he had been transformed by his experiences and was now returning to the tribe as a different person. This transformation was assumed—there was no obligation for a veteran to demonstrate that he'd suffered "enough," experienced "enough" trauma, or been through "enough" hardship to rate feeling different. He went. He did. And he was. That was all the tribe needed to know.

... the Vietnam veterans' combat experiences gave them a degree of knowledge about a subject few others are even conversant with; and because they are so knowledgeable, they obtain a certain degree of wisdom and respect. . . . A Winnebago elder . . . stated it best. . . . "We honor our veterans for their bravery and because by seeing death on the battlefield they truly know the greatness of life." (Holm, p.192)

But the veteran couldn't just come waltzing back into the tribe and pick up like nothing had happened. Holm describes the reasoning behind cleansing a returning warrior in the Cherokee tradition:

The Cherokee's personal bravery and service were cheered, but the war itself, simply because it was a war, was considered a particularly vile human activity. Since it was a vile experience and he was a relative, he had to be relieved of the terrible spell the war had placed upon him. Otherwise, the entire community could become tainted. Distributing the burden of his trauma thus became a community project. (Holm, p.193)

Far from being a "cure all" or magic ceremony to wipe away the effects of war, the tribal ceremonies were built around the concept that the warrior would never leave the trauma behind and would continually have to deal with it throughout his life. Holm uses a quote from Native American psychologists Don Johnson and Robin LaDue to explain how Native American medicine approaches recovery from trauma:

"It must be clearly understood, acknowledged and accepted that many of the healing ceremonies are not cures, but simply a part of the healing process provided through the entire community. The trauma is a point on the circle of life that must be passed through over and over again . . . It is recognized that each time one returns to the trauma point on the medicine circle there will be some deflection of the path. Here we depend upon the effects of past healing and repetition of appropriate ceremonial healing." (Holm, p.196)

These tribal traditions didn't spring up overnight. They weren't dreamt up in response to some newly perceived trauma associated with modern warfare. These rituals and ceremonies have been an integral part of tribal culture, handed down through the ages by men and women who understood their importance— and the repercussions of ignoring them. They reflect a deep societal understanding of the traumas experienced in war and offer the returning warriors relief without implying that they are weak for needing it.

But unless he or she belongs to a homogeneous society with established rites and rituals for guiding them home from battle, the modern warrior must navigate these treacherous waters alone. This is not to say our veterans are not given societal support, but rather that the support they receive has a different focus.

WHAT ABOUT THE SUPPORT WE *DO* HAVE?

The GI Bill, employment assistance, disability payments, and other federal benefits are available to most American veterans. The widespread societal support these programs enjoy acknowledges the sacrifices made by our service members and shows our nation's honest desire to provide real assistance upon their return. Where these programs fall short, however, is in focusing solely on the tangibles. Economic concerns are elevated to supreme importance among the list of challenges returning warriors face. It is as if gaining an education, learning a new skill, or getting a monthly disability check is all a warrior needs to make him whole, healthy, and stable.

While a good start, the benefits offered to our veterans are not comprehensive enough to address all of their needs. Missing are the means to reunite the conscious and unconscious minds and heal the disconnect between who the warrior *was* and who the warrior *is*. The veteran can learn skills and earn money, but if he or she is not at peace with their experiences, they will not be healthy and whole. They will not have come home.

This is not an indictment of the VA. That organization is working harder than ever to fulfill the nation's obligation to her veterans. But the VA cannot do it alone. Health care and economic support? Yes, it can provide those almost totally by itself. But guidance for addressing the full spectrum of war's impact? No, that will require a team effort by the individual veteran, various nonprofits, and the VA to be successful. Simply put, veterans must play a more active role in their own return than they have been told to expect. We must be the driving force behind our successful return and cannot outsource responsibility for overcoming our challenges to the VA.

Without established rituals and ceremonies that can help us close the chasm between our conscious and unconscious minds, the positive support our society can provide us is limited. There is definite value to the tangible support it does offer, but that support cannot go far enough. This isn't a fatal flaw in our system, but it does require us to compensate in ways we haven't been prepared for. It requires us to apply significant effort to understanding our experiences and reactions, get our own houses in order, and then, when our foundations are rock-solid again, make good use of the benefits our society *does* offer.

We have to marry the two concepts of societal support—inner and outer, spiritual and tangible. You're going to have to take care of the spiritual yourself.

Then, go claim the tangible.

5

THE VALUE OF MYTH

Wherever the poetry of myth is interpreted as biography, history, or science, it is killed. The living images become only remote facts of a distant time or sky. Furthermore, it is never difficult to demonstrate that as science and history mythology is absurd. When a civilization begins to interpret its mythology this way, the life goes out of it, temples become museums, and the link between the two perspectives is dissolved. . . .

To bring the images back to life, one has to seek, not interesting applications to modern affairs, but illuminating hints from the inspired past. When these are found, vast areas of half-dead iconography disclose again their permanently human meaning.

—Joseph Campbell, *The Hero with a Thousand Faces*, p.213

AS EXPLAINED IN THE LAST CHAPTER, war has the seemingly mythic ability to change a person. The chasm created by the different combat experiences of the conscious and unconscious minds fuels this change and persists long after we come home. Is this a new phenomenon? Something having to do with the speed and lethality of modern war? Or are modern warriors just more susceptible to it than their predecessors?

No.

War has always come home with those who fight. It echoes in our lives long after we've left the theater of combat as part of a basic human pattern. Understanding how deeply this pattern is ingrained in us is essential if we are to quiet these echoes and readjust to peace. It is an aspect of the warrior's journey we have been led to believe we can ignore if we are strong enough. The persistence of this false belief leaves us exposed to unnecessary, and predictable, suffering.

I say predictable because the challenges of coming home have been known for thousands of years. We see them reflected in modern works of art and literature but their origins run much deeper than that. These are universal human experiences that disparate civilizations throughout history considered important enough to enshrine in their cultural mythology. Joseph Campbell explains the value of this information in his book, *The Power of Myth*:

> These bits of information from ancient times, which have to do with the themes that have sup- ported human life, built civilizations, and informed religions over the millennia, have to do with deep inner problems, inner mysteries, inner thresholds of passage, and if you don't know what the guide- signs are along the way, you have to work it out yourself. (Campbell, p.2)

Myths can show us the archetypal warrior's journey. But they only provide general guidance for how to approach these uni- versal human experiences—not specifics. The details contained in myth are metaphorical representations of cultural beliefs and customs from ancient civilizations that may, or may not, be recognizable to us.

Does it help the modern warrior to know that Hercules knocked out the Twelve Labors and then, after returning home, killed his friend, accidentally killed a boy, then eventually got killed after shooting a centaur while it was raping his wife? Or that, after coming home bearing his prize, Prometheus had his liver ripped out daily by an eagle as punishment for stealing fire from the gods and giving it to his people? Or that Odysseus spent as long struggling to get home as he did in actual combat? No, the details are unimportant. What is important, however, is to note that the challenges these warriors faced did not end on the battlefield.

They followed them home.

But myths are valuable to us because we need their general guidance, first. Remember, we're still in the mission-planning phase of this operation. We're studying historical battles in the hopes we can learn something that will help us in the future. We need this background knowledge because we've only just now been informed these inner battles even exist. We've got some catching up to do before we can figure out what to do about them.

At this stage we need to conduct our reconnaissance—or as Campbell puts it in the quote that begins this chapter, to seek ". . . illuminating hints from the inspired past." The specifics of what we're facing can only become clear once we comprehend the archetypal warrior's experience as recorded in myths. The value of this reconnaissance is that, once we understand the full scope of the universal warrior's journey, it can show us where we've been and more importantly, where we need to go.

THE RETURN

The template of all the hero myths is simple: Separation, Adventures, Return. It is this final phase, The Return, that we must redefine. Modern warriors have been programmed to consider this to mean physically coming home, but as the final stage in a mythical warrior's journey, it goes far deeper than that. In myths, the warrior doesn't just melt back into society at the end of his journey. No, he returns to his original society with something of value gained as a direct result of his adventures in the unknown world. Campbell calls this the warrior's "boon."

In mythology, the warrior's boon is usually enhanced consciousness or a bit of "world-changing" knowledge gained in the course of the warrior's adventures. These adventures took him to a place beyond the normal spiritual realities of his world. They taught him things his society had either forgotten or never knew in the first place. The mythic warrior had, quite literally, seen and experienced things no other members of his society had—and thus learned lessons beyond the realm of *their* consciousness. His journey through this unknown world, and subsequent return with valuable knowledge, is what elevated him from adventurer to hero.

Why has the return been overlooked and ignored as part of our contemporary warrior tradition? Because the inner challenges of the return require the warrior to develop new strengths beyond those of the physical nature. Overcoming the challenges of the return requires spiritual growth, expanded consciousness, and self-awareness—areas not traditionally emphasized in our society's definition of a warrior. But whether we choose to embrace them or not, they are fundamental components of a healthy human mind. If we ignore their importance, we cease rising to the challenges of our journey. And as I mentioned before, if we refuse to face challenges then we stop moving forward. We stagnate.

WHO'S RESPONSIBLE?

Once we understand the general structure of the heroic monomyth, where do we get the details that can help us actually move forward? Without meaningful societal guidance in the form of ceremonies and rituals, how are we supposed to figure out how to keep from stagnating along our journey?

It would be nice if those details came to us in a flash of inspiration, or from a Yoda-like sage as they do in many myths, but that doesn't usually happen in real life. The reality is, the deeply personal nature of the challenges of coming home requires each of us to create our own ways to overcome them. Some of our methods might be similar, but the specifics and amount of effort depend solely on the individual. Figuring out those details is neither fun nor immediately rewarding. It takes serious effort, a willingness to face uncomfortable truths about ourselves and our experiences, and a high level of self-awareness.

The task of navigating the challenges of the return is complicated. And when you remove the guiding forces of culturally meaningful rituals and ceremonies, the task becomes even harder. This lack of specific guidance, societal pathways, and social understanding that warriors *need* to heal creates a situation that encourages stagnation. In our society, the answers for how to overcome the challenges of coming home are not provided to our warriors.

They—we—must figure them out for ourselves.

SOMEBODY'S GOT TO DRIVE

The bottom line is this: We each have to take responsibility for our own journey. Assistance is available, but we have to use it judiciously and recognize when it is—and is not—needed. We can, and should, delegate authority to the VA, to nonprofits, and to friends and family to assist us, but we can never delegate responsibility. We must be the driving force that propels us forward. Even if they wanted to, nobody can do that for us.

This may sound like a raw deal. Not only do we have to face all the physical challenges of combat, but now we also have to shoulder the responsibility for navigating the inner challenges as well? But who knows better than we do what we've been through? Who knows best what followed us home from combat? These are our lives, our challenges—and we're the ones best suited for the task.

Just as the specifics of each warrior's journey will be different, so will the type and amount of assistance each of us needs. What one veteran breezes past without a second thought may seem insurmountable to another. A moment's quiet reflection may be all that is required to regain your equilibrium—or it might take multiple visits to the Vet Center to restabilize. There is no single answer, and what works one day might not work the next.

It is possible, however, to come up with a plan of action for dealing with these challenges.

This plan, and any external assistance required, will change with time. In this regard, it is good that our system of support for veterans is dependent upon the veteran *asking* for it. This "a la carte" approach offers the veteran freedom to pick and choose what assistance, if any, he receives. He can try to work through challenges on his own, accept the maximum support offered, or choose anywhere in-between.

When considering how to move forward, it is important to realize that PTSD is not like being pregnant—you can have a little PTSD. Combat trauma is a term that describes experiences and reactions that cover this entire spectrum, from short-term adjustment challenges up to and including diagnosable PTSD. There are infinite gradations of combat trauma as well as infinite levels of reaction to it. The normal human reactions that end up meeting the clinical diagnosis of PTSD do not blossom instantly from zero to 100 percent. They grow over time, each small event or reaction adding to the overall accumulation of stress carried by the body and the mind. Many different, and poorly understood, factors determine if these reactions become diagnosable PTSD in a heartbeat, over fifty years, or never. The important thing to remember is that there is a long, long way between full-blown PTSD and being untouched by your experiences.

> Findings from the *National Vietnam Veterans Readjustment Study (NVVRS)* . . . showed that 35.8 percent of male Vietnam combat veterans met the full . . . diagnostic criteria for PTSD at the time of the study, in the late 1980's. . . . More than 70 percent of combat veterans had experienced at least one of the cardinal symptoms ("partial PTSD") at some time in their lives, even if they did not receive the full syndrome diagnosis. (Shay, *Achilles in Vietnam,* p.168)

If you think you may have full-blown PTSD, feel free to read the rest of this book after you've talked to your counselor about it. But don't assume my recommendations are a substitute for the assistance of a mental health professional. The recommendations in this book are more appropriate to veterans on the lower end of the PTSD scale, the area commonly referred to as "partial PTSD." Even minor wounds caused by combat trauma, if left unattended, can fester and become full-blown PTSD over time. But if we take the initiative to tend our wounds while they are relatively minor, then we stand the chance of healing them—or at least keeping them from getting worse.

Our entire system of support for veterans is based on the individual veteran taking the first step. This requires you, the veteran, to assess your status between "A-OK" and "AFU." You must triage yourself and make an honest assessment of how much damage you've sustained and how much danger you're in. Luckily, the same basic scale of treatment the military taught us for physical injuries can be applied to the invisible inner wounds of combat as well.

SELF-AID, BUDDY-AID, CORPSMAN-AID

The caustic emotions and deep-seated reactions generated by combat are often described as invisible wounds. This is an effective analogy because, like physical wounds, if left untreated they can go septic and spread into otherwise healthy parts of our bodies and minds. Treatment of these invisible wounds is also similar to that of physical ones—the more severe the injury, the more highly skilled the medical provider needs to be.

The Marine Corps teaches "self-aid, buddy-aid, corpsman-aid" as the sequence of medical support for physical injuries. A cut leg or sprained wrist—handle it yourself. A bullet through the calf—have a buddy put a pressure bandage on it. A sucking chest wound—"DOC!"

This concept of handling an injury at the lowest possible level should also be applied when considering how to employ the assistance that is available when coming home.

Self-aid is the first level of treatment. This is the heart and soul of any successful return and depends solely on the warrior to create and implement it. Properly planned by the individual, self-aid provides a solid starting point for a veteran's journey after combat. As that journey progresses, the self-aid plan can adjust and flex to meet the changing realities encountered. If there comes a time when self-aid isn't working, or simply needs a boost, help is available in the form of subclinical (buddy-aid) and clinical (corpsman-aid) support. But remember, a self-aid plan is essential if buddy- and corpsman-aid are to have any chance of being effective.

Buddy-aid is help that comes from friends, family, fellow veterans, clergy, or spiritual guides. It also includes the vast number of veteran-oriented nonprofits that have sprung up in recent years. Many of these nonprofits are designed around an experience that can provide an opportunity for participants to see their situation in a new light. A week of backpacking along the Appalachian Trail, a canoe trip in the Boundary Waters, or fly fishing on a secluded ranch can quiet the incessant interruptions of everyday life that inhibit reflection. During these experiences, and the quietude they offer, participants have the opportunity to gain a new perspective on the challenges they face.

Corpsman-aid, or medic-aid, means talking to a mental health professional. There are times when this is the first step a warrior must take—like when substance abuse, thoughts of suicide, physical abuse, or other negative coping mechanisms have already manifested themselves. If you are in that situation, don't screw around with self- or buddy-aid. Get to the doctors and allow them to apply the lifesaving steps you need. Once they have you stabilized, though, you have to come up with a self-aid plan to avoid ending up in that situation again.

LANGUAGE BARRIERS

Communications between people in different professions are difficult. Just like most of us can speak for several minutes using nothing but acronyms and cuss-words, the mental health professionals who make up the corpsman-aid level of treatment have a language all their own. This language is the standard for psychologists, psychiatrists, and counselors because they must uphold the standards of their professions. More importantly, these professionals use this clinical language because, amongst their peers, these words have very specific meanings. This is helpful when two shrinks are chatting about a patient's issues or describing specific treatment options. But when trying to encourage a combat veteran to understand what she's been through, and what is happening inside her head, this specialized language can be a hindrance. This is because the words used by mental health professionals often imply helplessness, weakness, or a sense of powerlessness—all characteristics that grate against the very fabric of most veterans' self-perception.

Throughout this book I use quotes from highly respected mental health professionals to support my points. Their recommendations and observations are written, however, using words that immediately make combat veterans say things like, "Victim? Hell, no. That's not me." Thus, valuable information may be tossed aside because a warrior cannot accept that what might apply to a victim of a crime could also apply to him. In the hopes that I can defuse this knee-jerk reaction, I offer the following alternate definitions:

> **Traumatic event:** Among mental health professionals, a traumatic event is defined as a powerful psychological shock that has damaging effects. Combat veterans experience them regularly and protect themselves from immediate injury using compartmentalization and gallows humor. Thus, we don't consider ourselves to have lived through a "traumatic event" when we see a vehicle get blown up. We react

in accordance with our immediate action drills and push through the kill zone. It sometimes takes a professional to explain to us how, exactly, the shock of that explosion affected us, because we're trained to assume it didn't. Glossing over "traumatic events" in order to accomplish our mission is just what we do.

Victim: Much of what is written about the effects of trauma uses this term. Victims of abuse, rape, terrorism, captivity, and other crimes often display the same symptoms and reactions as combat veterans. PTSD is not *our* issue, as veterans. It applies to victims of crimes and tragedy as well. While this term implies that the person is suffering PTSD because they were victimized—i.e., held powerless—this is not the case in combat veterans. None of us were *victimized* by our combat experiences. We readily and willingly went into the situations that are causing us pain. That's what we do—we're warriors—and we're not about to accept the label of "victim" when it is so obviously inappropriate. So, when you see that word, recognize why the professional used it—but don't let it turn you away from information you may need to overcome your challenges.

Survivor: This word holds much the same stigma as "victim." From the mental health professional's point of view, it's appropriate because few decisions made in modern war are actually made out of free will. Duty, orders, and legal requirements all limit the modern warrior's freedom of action. From that standpoint, it is understandable to imply that combat held us down and forced us into traumatic experiences. But from the warrior's standpoint, this is not the case. We knowingly accepted the trauma of combat as part of our duty and willingly agreed to limit the scope of our choices. That our preparation was inadequate to protect us fully from the effects of trauma is now obvious—but that doesn't make us feel like *survivors*. We're combat veterans, proud of what we accomplished in difficult situations. Whenever you see "survivor" used by a professional, just substitute "veteran" and push on.

Stressful Event: The *Oxford Dictionary of Psychology* defines stress as "Psychological and physical strain or tension generated by physical, emotional, social, economic, or occupational circumstances, events, or experiences that are difficult to manage or endure." (Andrew Colman, p.735)

This definition leaves every possible life experience open as a potential cause of stress, or as a "stressful event." But what might be a stressful event in a champion rose gardener's life—an infestation of slugs—would be laughable to a SAW[10]-gunner. But having his weapon jam in the middle of a firefight while all his buddies were relying on him to provide suppressive fire would certainly be stressful, maybe even traumatic depending on what happened next. The point is, the term "stressful event" sounds innocent and, well, just plain weak. We're warriors, we eat stress for breakfast. But the psychological community treats stress with much more respect and with good reason. This respect is reflected in the way they refer to stress in professional articles and books. When you see "stressful event" written

---

[10] SAW refers to the M249 Squad Automatic Weapon, a 5.56mm light machine gun.

in these books, substitute "shit I lived through that *really* pissed me off." This should keep you thinking about a double-feed on that damn SAW instead of oozy slugs eating pretty flowers.

THE DEVIL'S IN THE DETAILS

As I said in the beginning of this chapter, myths don't provide details for how to overcome the challenges of the return—they only assure us they are real and exert great power in our lives. In order to figure out these missing details, each of us must examine our own lives and experiences for clues. Motivations, methods of relaxation and excitation, recreational activities, lifestyles, relationships, and personal histories, all play a role in unwinding the emotions and reactions of combat. We just need to come up with a personalized plan for how to use them.

While the details depend on the individual, there is enough similarity among human beings as a species to allow for generalities. The aftereffects of intense experiences like combat fall into three categories: physical, emotional, and very often, spiritual. The body processes that enhance survival are common to all humans, as are the basic emotional reactions to stressful or traumatic experiences. Spiritual aftereffects have a bit more variance because spirituality and its concepts are generally learned, but there are enough commonalities across cultures and religions to make it a basic component that must be addressed by all returning warriors.

These three components—physical, emotional, spiritual— form the challenges of the return. They are what must be overcome for the warrior to achieve his or her boon and return to society whole, healthy, and wiser. It has been my experience that these challenges are best addressed in sequence: First the physical challenges have to be quieted, then the emotional chasm between the conscious and unconscious can be closed, and finally, supported by a calm body and mind, the spiritual concepts of right and wrong, good and bad, can be applied to actions taken—or not taken—in combat.

For each of these challenges, the concepts of self-aid, buddy-aid, and corpsman-aid apply. And for each of them, the requirement to create, execute, and monitor progress of the plan rests squarely on the warrior's shoulders. There is no quick-fix, and each veteran must resign him- or herself to a protracted campaign if they are to have a reasonable chance of victory. As Shay points out in *Achilles in Vietnam,* "Recovery from severe trauma more nearly resembles training to run a marathon than cathartic redemption in faith healing." (p.187)

So strap on your running shoes and get ready to get to work. No amount of wishful thinking, dancing with snakes or "speaking in tongues" is going to heal you instantly. These challenges are real, they're part of being a warrior, and defeating them requires a warrior's strength and courage. They are what stands between you and the rest of your life and overcoming them is going to be tough.

But nothing worthwhile is ever easy.

PART TWO:

COMPLETING THE

WARRIOR'S JOURNEY

6

GETTING PHYSICAL

AT THIS POINT I have to assume two things: First, that what I've explained about the warrior's journey, and how we're only prepared for some of it, makes sense to you and, second, that you're getting tired of background information. That information was critical to set the stage for the rest of the book—but I agree. It's time to start hammering out the details.

From here on out, the focus will be on the specifics. We will separate the challenges into their components, understand the support that is available to overcome them, and develop a plan to move forward. The remainder of the book will draw heavily on my experiences navigating my own, particular challenges. These examples are not meant as a prescription to be followed to the letter. I include them to illustrate desired effects, but they should be considered as only one of many possible routes through the challenges of coming home.

Because none of us have had the exact same experiences, your route will be different from mine. Our paths may overlap in parts or go in opposite directions, but they will likely share common components. The specifics of my journey are only important here because they explain *how* I addressed these common components. Understanding how the things I did worked for me is valuable knowledge that will help you figure out your own way forward.

STRATEGY

The challenges we face after coming home are not orderly and neat. They are a confusing mix of physical, emotional, and spiritual trials that hit us randomly and without warning. Sometimes, they hit all at once. This doesn't mean, however, that we should try to fight them all at the same time. Flailing out in every direction is never a good idea.

Instead, we must isolate the challenges, prevent them from reinforcing each other, and overcome them one by one. There's a sequence to taking them down that maximizes our effectiveness while degrading theirs, and each success gives us additional tools we can use to defeat the next. In *Achilles in Vietnam,* Shay describes the critical first step in this building block approach as establishing our own safety, sobriety, and self-care.

If safety, sobriety, and self-care create the stable platform required to move forward on our journey, restful sleep is the anchor that holds the platform in place. The remainder of this chapter will explore self- and buddy-aid options for building your own platform, as well as direct you toward resources for how to anchor it with solid sleep. If these suggestions don't work for you, though, corpsman-aid is just a phone call away. There are hotlines available—Veterans Crisis Line (1-800-273-8255) and the Vet Center's Combat Call Center (1-877-WAR-VETS), for example—that will connect you with a knowledgeable mental health professional 24/7, 365. They can serve as a gateway into other corpsman-aid options, but they can't come to you—you must pick up the phone and take the first step.

There may be a lot of alligators swimming around your boat, but they are not equal threats—it does no good to shoot the ones in the distance while the closest eats you. This chapter is going to focus on the one most likely to kill you first. Then we can turn our attention to the other sneaky bastards lurking farther away.

THE ALLIGATOR CLOSEST TO THE BOAT: PHYSICAL

> Survival skills, such as vigilant sleep, brought back into the civilian worlds of family and employment, are actually more destructive of the veteran's well-being than the intrusive persistence of the traumatic moment.

—Jonathan Shay, *Achilles in Vietnam*, p.175

The physical aftereffects of combat—irritability, jumpiness, hyper-arousal—are what people identify most with combat trauma. These reactions are made worse by a problem most veterans just assume is normal: We sleep like shit. Lack of restorative sleep exacerbates these physical aftereffects and hampers our ability to deal constructively with even normal, everyday stressors. While they may be the public face of combat trauma, these physical reactions are not its only components. Hidden beneath are the quieter, more subversive, emotional and spiritual challenges that erode us from within. But it is impossible to defeat those deeper challenges while suffering the tornado of physical responses to combat. These winds must be calmed, and restful sleep restored, if we are to find the quiet mental space required for self-awareness and introspection—two essential tools we'll need to overcome our emotional and spiritual challenges later on.

I'LL SLEEP WHEN I'M DEAD

One of the most crucial components of self-care is something that many veterans consider unimportant: sleep. Instead of treating sleep like a fundamental requirement to keep our bodies and minds functioning properly, our attitude toward this vital tool borders on contempt. We tell ourselves we don't need it, that we're strong enough to go without it, and that only the weak indulge in it. There may have been periods during our service when we simply had to go without sleep, but that time has passed. Now that we're home and facing new battles, re-establishing restful sleep should be one of our first priorities.

The negative effects of too little sleep on the human body and mind are well documented. Depression, anxiety, lack of concentration, impaired motor skills, and problems with memory are just some of the byproducts of not getting enough of it. This is an especially difficult problem for veterans to overcome because we consider being able to operate on minimal sleep a valuable skill. Training operations designed to simulate actual combat often purposefully deprived us of sleep in order to test us more fully. And actual combat? Forget about it. There may come a time when the military recognizes the value of well-rested warriors vice zombies and incorporates "sleep plans" into operational planning, but that is likely a ways off. Until that happens, most veterans leaving the service will do so without healthy sleeping habits in place. For us, restoring restful sleep must be one of the first continuing actions we accomplish after coming home.

One of the most common tools we use to help us fall asleep is alcohol. That's because it seems to work. We have a few drinks, get a little loose, then fall asleep almost as soon as our head hits the pillow. Or maybe we don't even make it to bed, passing out on the couch with the TV on. Alcohol gives us the impression that it's helping us sleep because we fall asleep faster. In actuality, we're shooting ourselves in the foot.

Alcohol keeps our brain from going into the Rapid Eye Movement (REM) stage of sleep—the stage where our brain is actively repairing and reorganizing itself. A normal, restorative sleep cycle will send us into and out of REM sleep multiple times per night. But when alcohol is in our system, this cycle is disrupted and we may never achieve REM sleep at all. We may be snoring on the couch for seven hours while the dog licks pizza grease off our face, but, when we do finally get up, our brain will be just as worn out as it was when we laid down.

But it will ruck up and keep going because that's what it's designed to do. Our brain will keep our heart beating, our lungs inhaling and exhaling, and we will continue to function, although at a reduced capacity. Our ability to manage complex thoughts, organize and access memories, and even conduct routine social interactions will be slowly, sneakily, eroded away. We might not even recognize this loss of brain function because chronic sleep deprivation has turned the part of our brain that would notice it—the frontal lobes—into a pile of mush. With the frontal lobes degraded by lack of sleep, injury, or drugs, operational control of our body passes to the lizard brain. This is the part of our brain buried at the base of our skull and, unless we're in a life-or-death situation, having it in full control of our actions is not a good thing.

The lizard brain regulates our basic survival mechanisms and doesn't need much sleep to function. This primitive part of our brain is pretty much hard-wired in the "go" position and, unless severed from the spinal column, will continue to keep our bodies doing all the things they need to do to survive. But the frontal lobes are different. They are used for higher-level thought and are constantly changing and reorganizing themselves—usually while we sleep. In addition to complex thoughts and providing ethical and moral restraint, the frontal lobes play a major role in keeping the lizard brain in check. This relationship gives us the ability to appreciate an attractive person nearby without immediately trying to rip their clothes off, or to remember that we don't have to fight every asshole we come across. The frontal lobes allow us to operate above the level of simply surviving and enable us to live in civil society. Restful sleep is critical to maintaining the appropriate balance between them and the lizard brain.

When we're not rested, though, the lizard brain gets a bigger say in how we behave. Unimpeded by conscious consideration, it bypasses the frontal lobes and dictates our actions without regard for repercussions. This is how we end up screaming obscenities at the jerk who cut us off on the highway, chasing him down, and getting thrown in jail for assault. This is what makes us react with rage to small inconveniences or disruptions to our plans and makes our family and friends fearful of what we might do next.

Lack of restful sleep makes every challenge harder to overcome. This is especially true when trying to transition back to normal life after combat because those challenges are directly reinforced by lack of sleep. It's almost as if every time we lie down, we're restocking the enemy's ammo for him.

The subject of sleep, and how to make sure we get enough of it to be healthy, is a branch of medical science too broad to cover here. While there are some basic sleep hygiene concepts that you can incorporate on your own, truly measuring the effectiveness of your sleep and figuring out how to improve it are best accomplished in consultation with a medical doctor. For a good description of the various self-, buddy-, and corpsman-aid options for sleep hygiene, take a look at chapter 4 of *Once a Warrior—Always a Warrior* by Charles Hoge.

WHERE THE TORNADO STARTS

Before we can calm them down, it is important to understand where the most visible aspects of combat trauma—the loud, boisterous, physical reactions to combat—come from. They are not symptoms of any sickness, disorder, character flaw, or weakness. Rather, they are normal, healthy human reactions to stressful situations. It is very likely they kept us alive and well while in combat and, during certain situations, will do the same for us at home. They're good, normal reactions—as long as they are situationally appropriate.

> The physical effects of PTSD on the body are indistinguishable from what happens as a result of extreme stress, but continue long after the source of the stress has passed. PTSD is essentially a manifestation of the natural mechanisms for survival and functioning under extremely threatening situations. Everything we label a "symptom" of PTSD is an adaptive and beneficial response when there is a threat to your personal welfare or that of others, and the persistence of these reactions is the body's effort to ensure that you're immediately ready if the danger occurs again. (Charles Hoge, *Once a Warrior—Always a Warrior*, p.35)

These "fight-or-flight" responses are hard-wired into our physiology. They are the human animal's turbocharger for use during times of danger. This turbocharger makes our heart rate increase, pumps adrenaline into our system, constricts our pupils for better focus, and floods our muscles with fuel. The speed at which our bodies make these changes in response to danger—perceived or real—is possible because of special pathways through our brains. These pathways give our primitive lizard brain the ability to instantly activate the tools needed for immediate survival without being hindered by conscious, rational thought. The frontal lobes are not part of these pathways. They're too slow, too hampered by reason and discretion to be effective survival mechanisms. That part of our brain gets "back-briefed" once the danger is past—if it's ever brought into the information loop at all.

In combat, these physiological responses to danger are appropriate and helpful. They give us the ability to focus on threats among chaos, drive our bodies to superhuman feats of strength and endurance, and maintain alertness beyond what we thought possible. We benefit greatly from having this turbocharger—but we don't get to control it. It turns on, and off, automatically. And the system is designed so that, if it fails, it fails in the "On" position.

But when the physiological processes of fight or flight do not automatically turn off, we have a problem. Operating at this extreme level places tremendous stress upon our bodies, and we are not capable of doing it for long periods without suffering serious adverse effects.

> Over time the combat veteran's body may seem to have turned against him. He begins to suffer not only from insomnia and agitation but also of numerous types of somatic symptoms. Tension headaches, gastrointestinal disturbances, skin disorders, and abdominal, back, or neck pain are extremely common. He may complain of tremors, choking sensations, or a rapid heartbeat. (Shay, *Achilles in Vietnam*, p.174)

In addition to hurting our overall health, severe reactions can disrupt every relationship in our lives—from everyday social interactions to personal relationships with those we love the most. In some cases, by the time a veteran returns home, the negative effects of these processes are already beyond the self- and buddy-aid options. When drugs and alcohol are being used to numb, when family members are physically afraid, or when risk-taking behaviors become uncontrollable, you must go straight to corpsman-aid. And fast.

But what if you're not in crisis mode? What if you're generally able to manage the excess energy, irritability, and unease without hurting yourself or others? The vast majority of us find ourselves in this position after coming home. We're never far from fight or flight, are always alert and quick to flash anger, but we're generally okay. Our coping mechanisms range from avoidance to denial and sometimes even give us a little relief. But we're aware that we're not operating as well as we could be. If you're in this middle ground—not "great" but not actively self-destructive either—you have the luxury of time. Use it to explore self- and buddy-aid options—or go straight to corpsman-aid if you want. External help is never a bad idea; it's just that some people prefer to handle things on their own. I know I did.

WINDOW ON MY WORLD

When I returned from Iraq after the 2003 invasion, I felt very different, uneasy and anxious. I was preparing for a second combat tour but as long as I was at work I felt fine. It was when I wasn't at work that I had a problem. It was impossible for me to relax, sit still, or even be fully present for a conversation with my fiancée. I was irritable and perpetually driven by an unquenchable need to do *something*. I always felt like there was someplace I needed to go, some task I had to accomplish. As I said, when I was at work that level of energy was appropriate—even welcomed. I worked hard and seemed a fountain of energy. But I couldn't turn it off.

I made a common mistake when I figured out what was going on—I poured a drink. It seemed to work at first, calming the ever-present need to do *something* and allowing me to relax after work. But then one drink didn't do it. Then two. Then three. I had embarked upon a path to alcoholism that was insidious and incredibly easy to fall into. If it hadn't been for my fiancée's timely intervention, I might have gone much further down that road than I did.

Because of her insistence, I stopped drinking as a means to dull my anxiety and irritability. Instead I turned to physical exercise, specifically free diving and spearfishing. I had always enjoyed being in the ocean, but these two activities gained a new importance for me after combat.

Being underwater provided a means to dissipate the excess alertness and energy my body's runaway turbocharger was pouring into me. In addition to being healthy exercise, stalking prey in the cold Pacific Ocean put me in a situation where the alertness and anxiety I felt were appropriate and helpful. I spent hours out in the kelp, hunting for food for as long as I could hold my breath. The knowledge that large sharks could be just out of sight in the murky water created a tingle of danger that I needed and welcomed. Being just beneath the "fight-or-flight" threshold was appropriate when I was underwater and, when I did finally come back to dry land, the excess energy was gone.

At first there was just a brief period after each diving session when I felt calm. After it dissipated, the anxiety returned. But the more I dove, the longer that period of calm lasted. Whatever physiological responses flying a Cobra gunship in combat had activated were slowly adjusting to the level required to keep me safe and alert underwater. After the incredible intensity of combat, my turbocharger had become stuck. It was outside my ability to turn it off, so I just had to let it run down on its own. Alcohol only numbed it, but diving gave me an outlet to flush that intense energy out of my system. It was a "stepping-down" process and, over time, the turbocharger turned off. I no longer *needed* to dive. But I still went anyway.

I didn't recognize what diving was doing for me at the time. All I knew was that I felt better—normal—after a good long session in the water. Luckily, my situation allowed me to escape underwater just about every day. Holding your breath and kicking 30-40' down in search of dinner might not be everybody's cup of tea, but it doesn't have to be. Each of us has some sort of activity we enjoy doing—we just have to make the effort to do it.

A WARNING

Many books about adjusting to life after traumatic or stressful events warn against "risk-taking" behaviors. Racing motorcycles on public highways, illegal base-jumping, and actively looking for physical fights are just some of the unhealthy—and downright stupid—ways we employ the excess energy created by our stuck turbochargers. But that doesn't mean that some risk taking is a bad thing. We just need to be smart about how we do it.

There is a certain amount of risk in everything. Simply flying a helicopter is dangerous. When you consider that military pilots dodge high-tension wires at night, in sandstorms, while people actively shoot at them, you can understand why a pilot's acceptable risk threshold is a little higher than the average person's. None of us *want* to die, yet we accept this risk in the routine execution of our duties because we're confident that our skills will keep us alive. Pilots are not unique in this regard and each military specialty has its own risks. Professional warriors mitigate them as much as possible but they cannot be eliminated. Some level of risk is a welcome part of a warrior's life—it makes things real, intense. And for some of us, it is a primary reason we joined up in the first place.

CONSIDERATIONS FOR EFFECTIVE SELF-AID

It is unreasonable to expect a returning warrior to forget the intoxicating sense of being *alive* that's created when death's a constant companion. But chasing it is a dangerous pasttime because it's a fleeting sensation that, once felt, requires more risk to achieve again. The trick, therefore, is not to quit the risk-taking activities cold-turkey, but rather to find an activity that provides a means to step down the intensity of the experience. You have to reset your excitement threshold to reasonable, healthy levels. The activity should be enough to give you the tingle of danger, not the intensity of actually dancing with death. You've done that and survived. You have nothing to prove by doing it again.

What are these activities? That depends—what do you like to do? Remember that promise about jumping out of airplanes? Here's your chance. Want to race motorcycles? Go ahead—just get professional instruction, do it on a racetrack, and get the proper equipment. Or maybe hunting will provide the tingle you need. Not exciting enough with a rifle? Try a bow—and hunt something with teeth. Look at the area you live in and explore the activities it supports. The options are endless, and it is up to you to discover what activity will sponge up your excess energy. Once you figure it out, don't be stupid. Get professional instruction, buy the appropriate protective equipment, and follow common safety practices.

There are some realistic limitations on what types of activities will work. It does no good if your chosen activity is too expensive or requires you to travel too far to do it. It needs to be something you can do close to home so you can do it often. And if you have to take out a loan to finance it, then you might want to reconsider your choice. The activity should also have a component of physical exercise, require a certain amount of concentration in order to do it safely, and offer a means to adjust the level of risk.

The physical exercise requirement doesn't have to be excessive. You don't have to run ultra-marathons in order for it to be effective. But it does need to be a component of your activity because exercise flushes stress from our bodies. Everything we bring home with us physically from combat revolves around stress. Not only do we have to face normal, everyday, life stressors that are challenging enough, but we also have to deal with the stress left over from our experiences in combat. On top of it all is the stress that comes from not knowing when and where disruptive emotions and reactions are going to hit us again.

This accumulated stress causes even the most easygoing among us to angrily explode in response to seemingly minor situations. Discipline and self-control keep our anger under wraps most of the time, but every once in a while an encounter with a rude driver, a whiny kid, or an inconsiderate passerby will cause us to lose it. This stress builds up within us and must be cleansed from our system—and exercise is a great way to do it. With the recent advances in adaptive sports, physical injuries that used to make exercise impossible for some veterans can be overcome. Skiing, swimming, kayaking, biking, and running are just some of the many sports conquered by veterans who've suffered amputations. So get outside, get your heart rate up, sweat, and feel your muscles cramp and burn. It's good for you.

Another component of a good activity involves mental participation. The leftover energy from combat often results in our brains running over the same experience or reaction again and again. We get no relief from the emotions of that experience and, instead of remaining in our past, they intrude on our present. But if the activity you choose requires you to concentrate on *it* instead, then your mind is given an opportunity to step back from the loop. This is another place where a little risk is a good thing. Risk, and the associated fear of screwing up and getting hurt, is a powerful motivator for focused concentration. Whitewater kayaking is a great sport for this, as are downhill mountain biking, skiing, surfing, boxing, and mixed martial arts, just to name a few. Any sport that provides physical exercise and requires mental concentration to do safely is a good choice.

The third aspect of a good sport is scalability of risk. Remember that the goal here is not to push the excitement and "rush" to new heights, but to slowly wean your body off the intense reactions of combat. To do this, the sport you select should allow you to adjust the level of risk in order to "step down" your body's physical responses to danger. Maybe you start racing motorcycles on a racetrack because your internal stress level demands the higher risks in order to feel balanced. But, when the internal energy has decreased a bit, maybe cruising on a Harley will provide all the risk and excitement you need. Kayaking might require big water and gnarly holes initially, but maybe a standing wave or even a flat-water paddle will calm your body and mind later on.

BUDDY-AID

But what if you don't have a sport or activity that you enjoy doing? What if you've never been an outdoor enthusiast and know nothing of that sort of recreation? Well, that's where buddy-aid comes in.

As mentioned before, there are literally thousands of non-profits and governmental organizations set up to provide outdoor recreation for veterans. Take a look at World T.E.A.M Sports (www.worldteamsports.org) for a good starting point to research what's available. Many of these organizations are centered on a specific activity—fly fishing, hiking, kayaking, mountain biking, horseback riding—and offer veterans of all ability levels a means to participate. They provide the gear, instruction, and all the logistics necessary to take you out of your current environment and teach you something new.

A great example of one of these organizations is the Wounded Warrior Patrol (www.woundedwarriorpatrol.org). Every year this nonprofit brings a group of wounded veterans and their families to a Pennsylvania ski resort for a week-long, all expenses paid, ski vacation. There is no requirement for previous skiing experience because most of the members of the Wounded Warrior Patrol are also National Ski Patrol instructors. The men and women who founded this organization donate their time and energy because they recognize the positive effects skiing has had on their own mental and physical health. They want nothing more than to give veterans access to the peace and tranquility of a day on the mountain, too.

This sentiment is not unique. Outdoor enthusiasts have created nonprofits to share the benefits of all types of sports. But they can't make us come to them—we have to search them out.

Getting veterans to apply for these programs is a challenge that frustrates many nonprofits. Often this is because veterans are loath to take a spot they feel another, more deserving, veteran should get instead. We tend to denigrate our own suffering by measuring it against other people's and deciding they are worse off. This mindset is part of our warrior ethos and is difficult to overcome—but we need to do it anyway.

Look at it this way. If everybody decided not to apply because someone else deserved it more, then these organizations would wither and die. Then nobody would have access to new sports and recreation—at least not the way these organizations offer it. The best thing for these groups is to have *too* many applicants. Then they can show their financial supporters how effective and sought after their program is—and how many deserving veterans are *not* able to participate for lack of funds. People who donate to these nonprofits want to know that their money will have a real impact, and hard numbers like that are solid gold for fund-raising activities.

The positive benefits of these activities continue indefinitely for the veteran community because buddy-aid goes both ways—you get help from a buddy, then turn around and offer it to another. Once you participate in an excursion or activity, you're in a position to share your experiences with other veterans. You can use the knowledge you gain from outdoor recreation with a nonprofit—be it technical skills, peace of mind, or both—to help your fellow veterans. Next time a buddy confides in you that he's having a hard time, you can invite him to join you on your next sport excursion. Or use your personal contacts in the nonprofit to hook him up. But before you can help him, you have to participate yourself. If you've taken the initiative to learn a new sport and realize its benefits, then you are in a good place to help your buddies do the same.

MONITOR YOURSELF

It's not enough to just pick a sport and go with it. It has to actually work for you. The best way to figure out if your chosen activity is effective is by monitoring yourself. Note your stress at various points throughout the day, using the activity as a reference point. Keep track of it on a notepad or in your smartphone. It doesn't have to be a big deal, just a few words describing how you're feeling before, during, and after your activity. A huge indicator of whether your activity is working is whether it improves your quality of sleep. Note if you feel more rested on days after doing this activity, and pay attention to what time of day you actually did the activity. If I went diving in the morning, then I usually slept better that night. But when I went night-diving, I had a harder time falling asleep afterward and my sleep quality suffered. Time of day matters when it comes to gaining the most from your activity.

This logbook is not for anyone else to see, so be honest. Recording this information will give you a means to look back and see patterns in how you are feeling and reacting—in relation to your activity. If the activity is effective, you'll see it in your log. If you can't see it, then maybe the activity isn't working for you. Choose another. Keep trying different sports, activities, or schedules until you find one that does work. This is individual effort and the only way to fail is to quit trying.

A HIDDEN TOOL YOU'LL USE LATER

In addition to ramping down your turbocharger, the physical activity you choose may have another, equally valuable, benefit: It may help you form meaningful relationships with new people.

Many of us feel isolated after leaving the service. While in the military we were constantly surrounded by intense relationships.

These friendships were based on trust and a shared sense of mission that gave them a depth few outside the military will ever know. But, despite promises to "keep in touch" after leaving active duty, we rarely do. A few phone calls and texts in the first few months home, then nothing. Paths diverge, daily experiences are no longer shared, and the ability to read each other's minds fades. Previously inseparable buddies drift apart as civilian life wedges itself between them. Special anniversaries become the only times we reach out and reconnect—and often only through Facebook or email. This may be a normal part of human relationships, but the fading of previously essential relationships strikes veterans at a very difficult time.

Combat is a life-changing experience. And as already discussed, coming home from combat is a tough life transition. It is cruel irony that at the moment we need friends the most, we become separated from them. But that is what happens when we come home. Some buddies stay in the military while others go back to their hometowns. Either way, we are left to face the challenges of our return alone.

But not if we make the effort to build new friendships. Many sports and activities have their own cultures and are almost clannish in nature. This is especially true for more risky, fringe activities popular with veterans. For example, folks who derive peace and tranquility from jumping out of perfectly good airplanes are birds of a feather, so to speak. The similarities they share usually go beyond the simple enjoyment of parachuting and provide a base for real friendships to develop. It is quite likely that you'll find other veterans who also participate in the sport you choose. Finding someone who enjoys the same recreational activities you do, lives relatively close by, and who may be dealing with similar challenges of coming home is like winning the lottery. The value of friendships like that cannot be overstated—especially considering the emotional and spiritual challenges to come.

Friendships are nice to have while calming the physiological aftereffects of combat, but they become vital when we move on to the next challenges. Dealing with the emotional and spiritual aspects of coming home is not something you want to face alone. Nobody should have to—or can—go through this alone. Sometimes a friend makes all the difference. True friendships do not sprout up overnight, however, and must be cultivated over time. Your military buddies will drop everything in order to answer your call for help, but solid friends you see every day can keep you from needing to make that call. A nonchalant phone call to coordinate an afternoon bike ride can lead to conversations between friends that have the ability to defuse a situation before it develops into a crisis. That's why it is important to form these relationships now, amidst the camaraderie of physical recreation, before you move on to the next stage of your return.

THE NEXT STEP

Having an activity that reduces stress, results in periods of physical and mental calm, and provides healthy interaction with people is valuable for anyone. The same is true for the ability to get regular, restful sleep. But for a warrior intent on moving through the challenges of returning home, these tools are not luxuries. They're essential. And the value of balanced activity and rest does not end when your turbocharger has reset itself to normal levels.

Depending on where you fall on the spectrum, quieting the physical aftereffects of combat might be the final task you must overcome. Or it might be just the beginning. How can you tell if your challenges are complete? The periods of quiet you experience after your activity will tell you.

These periods of respite won't last long at first. The more time you spend in an activity that sponges up your excess energy, however, the longer the calm period afterward.

IN MY OWN EXPERIENCE

At first, my calmness lasted only as long as it took me to stop shivering from my dive—then the irritability and anxiousness would sneak back in. But over a period of months, those comfortable periods lasted longer and longer until, finally, my normal state of mind wasn't dominated by getting mad at the drop of a hat or by a constant need to be doing something. I had a healthy coping mechanism in place that was effectively dissipating my excess energy from combat. Instead of signaling the end of my challenges, however, getting the physical reactions under control showed me there were more to come.

Once the loud, physical aftereffects were under control, I noticed signs that my journey was still incomplete. I didn't want them to be there, but, in the absence of the irritability and anxiety that used to mask them, their presence became unmistakable. I began to feel fundamentally uneasy with myself—like I didn't know who I was anymore. The concept I held of myself before combat no longer fit reality. I didn't know *how* it had been changed, only that it had been.

This realization ushered me into the next phase of my return—the emotional and spiritual challenges of coming home. Calming the physical was the necessary first step that established my own personal safety.

But it was only the first step.

7

EMOTIONS, SHIT

Narrative can transform involuntary reexperienc-
ing of traumatic events into memory of the events,
thereby reestablishing authority over memory.
*Forgetting combat trauma is not a legitimate goal
of treatment.*

—Jonathan Shay, *Achilles in Vietnam*, p.192

IF YOU HAVE ESTABLISHED your own safety and sobriety,
either through self-, buddy- or corpsman-aid, then you are ready
to move forward. The next challenge you must overcome is figuring out how to reestablish authority over your own memory
because, even if you don't remember these experiences, you can't
forget them.

Great, that's super helpful. So how the hell are we supposed
to go about making sense of something we can't even consciously
remember?

By telling our own true narratives.

Sounds deceptively easy. But in reality, understanding our
experiences thoroughly enough to be able to communicate them
to another person requires a lot of hard work. It is this hard
work, unpacking the emotions generated by our experiences,
that creates a pathway through the emotional challenges of the
warrior's return.

We're at a disadvantage with these challenges right from
the start, mainly because we don't want to admit we even feel
emotions, let alone that some are so powerful as to overwhelm
us. There was something almost heroic in facing the physical
challenges. But emotional ones? How the hell am I supposed to
make that sound tough?

I'm not. So get over it. This shit is real, it can really destroy you and your family, and you have to get over this hang-up about "emotions" and move on. This chapter will explore the reality of the warrior's emotions and the dangers of ignoring them. Emotions are part of being human, even for tough guys and gals. It's time we learned how to deal with them.

WHY?

Why should we go through all the trouble to unpack and process painful memories and emotions? Why can't we just leave them packed away in the dark corners of our minds and ignore them? Stack them up, lock the door, and put HAZMAT signs all over. Why can't we just let sleeping dogs lie?

Because they're not sleeping.

Remember the chasm formed by compartmentalization? The one created when our unconscious mind experienced the full brunt of our emotional reactions in real time while our conscious mind was protected? This chasm, created by the unequal experience of intense emotions, does not lie dormant. Until we close it, this chasm will make us uncertain of our emotional responses.

How many times have you expected to feel one emotion—only to get waylaid by another? This is the result of the split between our conscious and unconscious minds and leads us to distrust our own emotional stability. Unruly, unpredictable emotions follow us home from combat and, through us, impact our families. These weird flashes of intense emotions are often the most visible indication that combat changed us. But because we don't understand them, we grow ashamed of their existence. They become something we must hide, must suppress, must ignore—or else admit to something that feels like weakness.

But even if we successfully compartmentalize our emotions, we can't catch them all. Experiencing one emotion might allow another, totally unrelated, one to sneak out. A moment of parental bliss can be the Trojan horse that allows hidden memories of Iraqi children begging for MRE packets to escape. Who wants to remember the guilt felt at ignoring their pleas for food or annoyance when they pressed too close to the Hummer? Maybe that packet of hard candy didn't have to be thrown so hard to drive them back. What if somebody hit my kid like that? . . .

The reality is, we can't pick and choose what emotions to cut off to protect ourselves from these flashes—we have to control them all. If we revert to compartmentalization, we must put the tourniquet back on and crank it down tight. In doing so we choose to deny all emotions rather than suffer unpredictable flashes of anger, sadness, fear, or guilt. We grow cold, emotionally distant, and always on guard against a part of us we neither trust nor understand.

This is the easy road to take. All we have to do is revert to what worked in combat and tighten down control of our emotions. But the cost of wearing that tourniquet is a life of ruined relationships with friends, lovers, spouses, and children. It cuts off not only painful emotions and memories but the good ones as well. We deny ourselves opportunities for true joy and happiness—even the basic experience of being alive—for the remainder of our time on earth. We become shells of people at that point, incapable of creating and maintaining the emotional connections essential for human happiness.

> Because post-traumatic symptoms are so persistent and so wide-ranging, they may be mistaken for enduring characteristics of the victim's personality. This is a costly error, for the person with unrecognized

127

post-traumatic stress disorder is condemned to a
diminished life, tormented by memory and bounded
by helplessness and fear. (Herman, p.49)

Is this the burden we, and our families, must bear? Must
our families forever hide their pain and confusion at our actions
behind a shield of "We don't know—he was never the same
after the war"? Are we "condemned to a diminished life" where
neither we, nor anybody else, can understand why we react the
way we do?

No. There is another way.

DIFFERENT BATTLE, DIFFERENT TACTICS

If continued compartmentalization maintains and possibly
widens the chasm, then *de-compartmentalization* is the key to
closing it. This means that what we stuffed away and ignored
in combat must be pulled out and experienced now. To accomplish this we must change our tactics: Instead of closing down,
we must open up, instead of tightening the tourniquet, we must
take it off. The dark chambers in our minds must be opened, the
contents within examined, and the formerly trapped emotions
given the chance to run their course. We must allow ourselves to
consciously experience *now* what we couldn't *then*.

Roy Grinker and John Spiegel were psychiatrists who worked
extensively with soldiers during and after WWII. During that
time, hypnosis and narcosynthesis (the use of sodium amytal to
induce an altered state) were being used to gain access to veterans'
hidden traumatic memories. While those methods were effective
in retrieving traumatic memories, they did not effectively reduce
the symptoms of what would later be labeled PTSD.

Grinker and Spiegel observed likewise that treatment would not succeed if the memories retrieved and discharged under the influence of sodium amytal were not integrated into consciousness. The effect of combat, they argued, "is not like the writing on a slate that can be erased, leaving the slate as it was before. Combat leaves a lasting impression on men's minds, changing them as radically as any crucial experience through which they live." (Herman, p.26)

It's not easy to uncover these memories. Our walls of compartmentalization are solidly built, and we often don't even know what's hidden behind them. To top it off, we place great value on those walls because they protected us in combat. Let's face it—we *liked* being able to focus on our mission amid chaos. We took pride in the fact, rightfully so, that others could count on us in a crisis. Those walls made us feel good on some level, almost indestructible, and we are loathe to discard the protection they offer. But that protection has served its purpose and is no longer needed. Clinging to it like a security blanket only traps us in the past.

If you've quieted the physical aftereffects of combat and are not actively destroying yourself with drugs, alcohol, or unmitigated risk-taking, then you've achieved the goal of the first stage of healing: Safety. This is a good start but it's time to get moving again.

SELF-AID: THE BACKBONE OF YOUR STRATEGY TO MOVE FORWARD

Just as they worked for overcoming the physical challenges, the concepts of self-, buddy-, and corpsman-aid apply to the challenges of uncovering, understanding, and communicating the emotional reactions to combat as well. Various counseling methods offered by the VA make up the corpsman-aid level of support. Even if you do immediately talk to a counselor, though, remember that he or she is not the Happiness Fairy. You bear the ultimate responsibility for healing your wounds and must go into counseling willing to do the hard work required for it to be successful.

Regardless of whether you work with a counselor or not, you must develop and apply your own self-aid efforts to work through your emotional backlog. The external support offered by buddy- and corpsman-aid options should be considered supporting arms. You can call on them for assistance, like close air support or artillery, but don't expect them to win the battle for you. External support is effective only if there is an underlying plan to support. The simple fact is, *you* must be fully dedicated to emotional self-aid before any amount of buddy- or corpsman-aid can help.

The self-aid plan I'm going to lay out provides a means to dig these memories and emotions out of their hidden positions. But following it is not going to be easy or comfortable. It will demand personal courage on your part because it cannot be done from inside a bunker. You must abandon your protection, break down the walls of compartmentalization, and share what you've been through. There's simply no other way.

IMMEDIATE SHARING—IT JUST DOESN'T WORK

When I first got home from Iraq, I attempted to tell people what it had been like. Family, friends, acquaintances, well-wishers on the street—it didn't really matter who. I just wanted them to understand what I'd been through. I'd been to a realm of human experience that was terrifying, fascinatingly fantastic, and undeniably real. I'd done things that had profound impacts on me and I wanted people to know what they were. Problem was, I didn't know what they were myself.

I hadn't done any of the legwork required to understand what I'd been through, and my inept attempts to explain my experiences frustrated the hell out of me. I couldn't find the words to adequately describe the intense reactions I'd had in combat. It was too cumbersome to try and explain how I could simultaneously feel pride and horror at killing another human being. Or how the crushing fatigue of eighteen hours in the cockpit could be erased by a moment of terror—only to come crashing back seconds later. I was trying to tell people things I'd hidden behind my walls of compartmentalization, but I didn't really know what they were.

I found myself struggling for words, grasping at half-formed analogies, and was constantly interrupted by the realization my words sounded like a weak Hollywood script. The blank stares, polite nods of encouragement, and general statements of thanks told me the person I was talking to had no clue what I was trying to say. So I stopped trying.

This is not uncommon. Among veterans I've talked to, it seems there is a period of time when most of us try to share what we experienced—only to have the attempts end in failure. Instead of rebounding and trying a different approach, though, we usually quit right there. We feel a vague sense of shame that we even *tried* to share our experiences and a sharper pang of confusion when we realize we were unable to do so.

These initial failed attempts at communication reinforce the idea that we should just bottle it all back up and stuff it away. We convince ourselves there is no point trying to share because nobody could possibly understand anyway. But there is a point, and a very tangible benefit to our families and ourselves if we can share this information. It's not going to be as easy as just blurting it out, though. We have to close the chasm first.

THE FIRST STEP IS BRIDGING THE GAP

Compartmentalization created the chasm between your conscious and unconscious minds. To close it you must bring your conscious mind up to speed. This requires you to open hidden compartments, release the intense emotions trapped inside, and gain perspective by being able to see the entirety of your experiences. The eventual goal is to be able to effectively communicate what you've been through to another person, but that is impossible if you don't first understand it *yourself*.

To become conscious of the information you'll eventually need to share, you must first excavate it from hidden compartments in your mind. Good counselors can help you do this, but there is a lot you can do yourself. Self-aid for this stage demands a deeper, more multifaceted process of self-discovery than verbal communication normally offers. For me, this situation required writing.

Writing offers us the ability to lay everything out before us, edit, cut out, add, and work through layers of often conflicting emotions. Some of these emotions are loud and obscure the quieter, more-nuanced emotions that feed our vague sense of unease. But by moving them outside our heads and onto paper, we can quiet the boisterous emotions and become aware of what lies beneath them. Writing is also slower than speaking and gives us the ability to remain inside a memory long enough for it to fully bloom in our comprehension. This forces us to slow down and prevents us from skipping over important events we might otherwise unconsciously avoid. And if we can get to the point where what we've written is an accurate portrayal of how we truly felt during those experiences, then our conscious mind will have been brought up to speed along the way. The writing process will have steeped it in the same emotions the unconscious was exposed to in combat, and the chasm will be closed.

I'd been working on my first book for several years before I saw how writing had done this for me. I did not choose writing as part of any master plan, just as an honest desire to get to the bottom of what was bothering me. I eventually did just that, but the road I took held many unneeded twists and turns. When those are removed, the process becomes much more straightforward—and the chances of success that much greater.

OPS PAUSE

Hold where you are. No plan survives first contact with the enemy and adjustments are inevitable. There is danger involved with excavating the emotions and reactions of our past without first having the right support structure in place. Mental health professionals are adamant that trying to dig them up *before* we have established a framework for safety and support is dangerous. This is not a test to see who can pull out the nastiest memory the quickest or to see who's strong enough to handle it. Some memories need to be treated like the HAZMAT they are.

This is a good point to stop and take an honest self-assessment. Just like you'd check yourself for broken bones before gathering your parachute and trotting off the drop zone, now's the time to evaluate if you're ready to move ahead—or if it's time to call in the Doc.

Are you stable? Do you have healthy, supportive relationships with friends and family? Is the physical activity you chose sponging up the leftover physiological reactions to combat? Remember, this is not something you do once and then you're done with it. You'll need to continue to use this activity in order to gain the quiet periods in which to address the deeper, more nuanced emotional reactions to combat. These quiet periods are essential to establishing your safety and sobriety and must be in place before you can progress to the next level of healing.

SPEED IS *NOT* OF THE ESSENCE

If you're not there yet, don't rush it. Take advantage of this pause in operations to consolidate your gains in the form of personal safety and sobriety before moving forward on your journey. This includes assessing your relationships and making sure they are healthy and supportive. More than one veteran has been side-tracked by relationships with people who encouraged stagnation by actively working against their efforts to heal. Have a buddy who just wants to get wrecked every night? Or a romantic partner who demands that you "get over" whatever is bothering you so they won't be inconvenienced? Recognize these relationships as dangerous and insulate yourself from them as needed. Not everybody who knew you before combat will be capable of helping you afterwards.

The dangers of advancing into painful and confusing memories without first creating a secure environment may make it worthwhile for you to talk to a mental health professional—even online or through a 24-hour hotline—before driving on. Doing this can help you accurately assess how good your support structure is and whether you're ready to move forward.

Just accepting the challenges of coming home has put you on the right path. This path is neither a straight line nor easy to follow, however, and requires careful self-discipline and awareness of potential threats to travel it safely. Luckily, this race is not against the clock.

In this race, progress is ensured by the absence of stagnation. The distance each of us must travel is different, and some journeys are significantly longer than others. How long it takes is irrelevant. Any movement forward, no matter how small, puts you closer to *really* coming home. It may seem like slow going, but as long as you've established your own safety, sobriety, and self-care, time is on your side.

By refusing to stagnate, you have already taken the hardest step in any journey—the first one. So don't worry about the clock. Things will change, they will get better, and you will move forward—and the next chapters will show you how.

8

KUM BAY YAH, ANYONE?

In the second stage of recovery, the survivor tells the story of the trauma. She tells it completely, in depth and in detail. This work of reconstruction actually transforms the traumatic memory, so that it can be integrated into the survivor's life story.

—Judith Lewis Herman, *Trauma and Recovery*, p.175

TO UNDERSTAND THE EMOTIONAL effects of your experiences, you must tell your own true narrative. Don't get freaked out—this isn't some New-Age, self-help catch phrase, and it isn't going to require joining a drum circle.

Your own true narrative is simply your story—what you saw, did, didn't do, heard, smelled, tasted—and how it made you feel. That's it. How does this help you to move forward on your journey? By bringing the events, actions, emotions, and reactions of combat into the light. Only after these insurgent forces have been brought out of the darkness can they be consciously assimilated into your life.

There doesn't have to be a moral to this narrative or some underlying theme that ties it all together. You may find that, you may not. There is only one thing this narrative must contain and that's the truth. This is not the time to consider what you think people *want* to hear or how you *want* them to see you. Incorporating those external considerations will reduce what could be a crucial step forward in your journey to just a throwaway story—something to tell a stranger at a bar. A story like that hinders progress and encourages stagnation, the exact opposite of what your own true narrative will do for you.

It is important to remember the goal of this first step. You are not writing a book or a journal for other people to read. This is just for you. You may choose to share it later, but this first round of excavation is meant to simply pull all the emotions and reactions out of the darkness to give you a chance to make sense of them yourself. Once you've accomplished that, you can decide whether or not to share what you discovered and the means through which to share it.

The value in telling your own true narrative is in the journey it takes to learn it. That's what we're going to talk about here.

GATHERING THE INTEL

I have a hard enough time remembering what I did last week, let alone years ago. Our memories fade over time, and often our combat experiences seem to morph together into one long period. Memories that, at the time, felt scorched into our souls somehow become hard to recollect. Details slip away and events become jumbled up together like so many writhing snakes, seemingly impossible to separate. As a result, we usually associate our combat experiences with broad-brush emotions that are incapable of carrying the nuances we'd actually felt.

Combat isn't a uniform experience. There are good times, shitty times, and times that fall somewhere in-between. If we are to understand how various events impacted us, we have to make them—and our reactions to them—stand alone from all the rest. We need to tie our reactions to specific events as opposed to the entirety of a deployment or career. But because of the way our minds work, extracting the details of past events, especially traumatic ones, can be very difficult.

> Traumatic memory is not narrative. Rather, it is
> experience that reoccurs, either as full sensory

140

replay of traumatic events in dreams or flashbacks, with all things seen, heard, smelled, and felt intact, or as disconnected fragments. . . . In other instances, knowledge of the facts may be separately preserved without any emotion, meaning, or sensory content. (Shay, *Achilles in Vietnam*, p.172)

Even locating the memories and emotions of our experiences in combat can be a challenge. But, we can circumvent our mind's attempts to keep us from accessing that information if we develop, and stick to, a plan.

SELF-AID: DE-COMPARTMENTALIZATION[11]: STEP ONE

The first step in the process of constructing your narrative is to create a list of events that occurred during your deployment(s). These will likely be the "big" ones—the date you arrived in country, your R&R, major operations, noteworthy firefights, holidays, the day a buddy was killed—and will form the framework of your deployment(s) so you can begin filling in the gaps. Get a calendar, or make one, and put any remembered occurrences on their actual dates.

A whole lot of stuff happened between those dates though. Now you have to figure out what those more minor events were. Use the "big" events as a trail of breadcrumbs to follow backward into your memories. Jot down smaller events in relation to the bigger ones—before or after—and don't necessarily worry about the actual dates.

Of course, if you kept a diary, then use it. If you kept mission notes or a debrief logbook to record information for intelligence

---

[11] A condensed "De-compartmentalization Checklist" is included at the end of this book in Appendix A.

reports, then use them. Anything that you wrote during that time frame is valuable here. I used my own journal, my kneeboard cards from actual missions, my flight-hour logbook, and hours of gun-camera footage from my helicopter to rebuild my experiences while writing *After Action*. I plotted grid coordinates of various incidents and engagements on GoogleEarth and recreated as much of the aerial control point system as I could. You're trying to reconstruct something that happened years ago, and each bit of information is a puzzle piece. Pulling together as many puzzle pieces as possible gives you the best chance of actually creating a cohesive picture.

This is an opportunity to call in a little buddy-aid as well. Reach out to former comrades and use them to help rebuild your memories. Maybe they remember things you don't, or maybe they kept a journal and will share it with you. I was able to borrow my co-pilot's journal and found that he had recorded things I'd missed. Even more important than just gathering information, though, were the conversations it started. I couldn't just ask, "Hey dude—could I borrow your journal from Iraq?" I had to explain what I was doing, why I was doing it, and what I hoped to get from accessing his memories. This request for support broke an unspoken agreement to never admit any confusion or difficulty over what we had done. It was as if we believed our emotions could be ignored out of existence by not mentioning them. But asking to borrow his journal finally broke that foolishly naive pact. We'd fought in multiple engagements together, buried good friends, and have been best friends for years. But I had to take the first step and admit that something was bothering me before we began to have honest conversations about how those experiences actually impacted us.

DE-COMPARTMENTALIZATION: STEP TWO

Once your personal deployment calendar contains some solid information, it is time to move to the next step. Get a 3-ring binder with loose-leaf paper in it. Dedicate a sheet of paper to every date you've marked on your calendar and write what happened on that date. Begin with the bare facts—the who, what, when, where, and why of the event—just like you're going to turn it in for an after-action report. If anything else comes to mind then record that as well. Don't force it though; move on to the next significant event on a different sheet of paper if you get stuck.

This first recording of events will likely jog your memory. Each event initially exists in isolation in your mind, but the effort of recording the details forces you to examine that event closely. In doing so, other events linked to these primary ones may pop up in your memory. Capture them and write their details on their own sheet of paper. The goal here is to impose a basic level of organization on the memories jumbled by compartmentalization so that you have a thorough, tangible record of your experiences in combat.

Now it's time to go back through that binder and add another layer of information. This is the tough part—remembering and recording emotions created by those events. But don't worry; nobody ever needs to see what you write here. This notebook is simply your tool to use, your place to dump the memories and emotions extricated from the compartments in your mind.

Go back through your binder a few times with an eye toward what these events made you feel. Underneath the bare facts of each event, write the reactions that come to mind. They can be from the day itself, or how you are feeling right then and there as you think about it. Either way, you are accessing the compartmentalized reactions created by the event and jotting them down on paper—they can't be stuffed away again. That's not to say that you'll experience everything again in a rush. The walls of compartmentalization are solidly built and will not allow much to escape. But each little bit that does get out is a step in the right direction.

Flashes of compartmentalized emotions that do escape, if not recorded, usually get recaptured and stuffed away again by our conscious mind, thus ensuring they will escape again in the future. But writing them down circumvents this re-compartmentalization reaction and gives the emotions a place to live outside your head.

You may have to go through this process multiple times. If you can't remember how you felt at a certain event, try to remember what your body felt like. Did your teeth hurt from gritting them for so long, or your hands ache from crushing your weapon? Was your heart racing even though you weren't doing anything physical? Our bodies react to emotions even when we successfully compartmentalize them. Recalling those physical sensations can provide important clues to remembering the emotions that caused them.

It is quite possible that, during the process of remembering and recording the events and emotions of the past, you'll find yourself experiencing those emotions in "real time" again. Be aware that this can happen and prepare for those emotions to interrupt and intrude in your daily interactions. Ramp up your self-aid activities, use buddy-aid by letting friends and family know what you're doing so they can help, and always keep the door open to seeking corpsman-aid. Uncovering a memory that requires immediate corpsman-aid is not a bad thing. Quite the opposite. It means that you can go to your first meeting with your counselor with a concrete starting point. This can literally save you hours of sifting through memories and events to uncover the root cause of your unease.

Back to the second step of de-compartmentalization.

Another good tool to use in this stage is the correspondence with friends and family—more buddy-aid. Letters and emails we sent back from the war zone often contain hints of our emotional state at that time. But we may not have written our true emotions down—we usually wrote what we *wanted* them to be, not what they were. I remember sending my then-girlfriend, now wife, a letter after one mission on the ground in Baghdad. The breaching charge we placed on the front door of the target house blew just as a woman inside was reaching for the handle. She took the brunt of the blast, and the door broke her nose when it flew off its hinges.

After we'd secured the house and captured our target, she refused to allow our corpsman to give her medical assistance. Our "Terp," an Iraqi American from Detroit, dismissed her with a casual wave when she launched into an angry tirade from behind a mask of streaming blood. In the letter to my girlfriend, I angrily berated this woman for being such an idiot. We didn't want to hurt her; she should have kicked her dickhead husband to the curb for planting IEDs and then we wouldn't have had to blow her door in and wreck her house. It was her own damn fault, I wrote. Truth was, I felt like shit that this woman had been hurt by our actions—even more so because I did nothing to help. I just focused on my job and got to the roof where I could control the aircraft protecting our small force. Reading the misplaced anger and total confidence in my perceptions of right and wrong in that letter now makes me cringe.

The emotions we wrote in those letters will often ring hollow if they're not really what we'd been feeling. This hollowness is apparent only to us because our unconscious mind shouts "Bullshit!" when we read our words from years ago. This is a clue telling us that we should pay attention. This hollowness is our unconscious telling us we're on the right track, that we need to dig deeper here to uncover buried emotions. These are the ones leeching poisons into our emotional groundwater. They're what we're looking for.

We might write about feeling angry at the Iraqis for using kids as shields or bombers, but what we're really angry about is the fact that they put us in a position where we had to kill kids— or even contemplate it. Aggressive professions of our inherent "goodness" are often used to cover up the painful realization that we are neither as good nor as altruistic as we claim to be. This is especially true when we can look back and see how much pain we caused while simultaneously knowing, without a shadow of a doubt, that we'd done the right thing at the time.

The truth is, few people are more likely to experience the full disillusionment of smashed ideals than a warrior in combat. Ideals created and nurtured in peacetime rarely survive the ugliness of human combat. And as these ideals often define what's right and wrong, when they are crushed by the harsh realities of war, the warrior's concepts of right and wrong get crushed as well.

There's no time limit for gathering this information. It will take as long as it needs to take. But over time, your binder will contain the facts about your experiences and the general emotions they created. By giving them a place to live outside your head, you'll defuse their incessant escape attempts—the emotions will calm down and you'll be ready to move to the next step. You're closing the chasm by this point, but you're not done yet. You still have to gain perspective on the entirety of your experiences—not just individual events. To do that will require, you guessed it, more writing.

DE-COMPARTMENTALIZATION: STEP THREE

> The recitation of facts without the accompanying emotions is a sterile exercise, without therapeutic effect. As Breuer and Freud noted a century ago, "recollection without affect almost invariably produces no result."
>
> —Judith Lewis Herman, *Trauma and Recovery*, p.177

Get something fresh to write on. Could be a journal, a notebook, or a computer—whatever you're most comfortable with. This is the stage where you are going to put all your previous work together and connect the emotions and events into a single narrative or story. Start at the beginning event, the first page in your 3-ring binder, and write out what you did, where you did it, who you did it with, what it felt like, and how you feel about it now. Include all the emotions you can remember, and spend time on the details. It can literally take days to uncover the emotions and reactions generated by a single event. Go from significant event to significant event, filling in the gaps with any additional information that comes to mind. It may read like an overly personal after-action report, it may read like stream of consciousness, or it may read like a novel. It doesn't matter what it reads like. All that matters is that you spend the time and energy required to get it right.

If writing is not something that comes easily to you, don't worry—buddy-aid is available for this, too. You've done the hard work to collect all your raw material; now you just need some help organizing it.

At this point in my own journey, I had the good luck to stumble upon David Hazard, founder and director of Ascent, an international coaching program for authors, and the man who would become my writing coach. I'd already written the first draft of *After Action*—over 420 pages of who-what-when-where details—when we started working together. While it was essential for me to write that first draft, it was nothing anybody else would ever want to read. It was just for me, an opportunity to put my experiences on paper and organize them outside my head. Actually, the writing was crap, devoid of emotions and personality. I would have to delve much deeper into *how* my experiences had affected me if it was to have any hope of becoming a book, even though at that time, I wasn't certain I wanted it to.

I was not an easy client for David. I was so wary about admitting I even had emotions that any attempt by him to get me to describe how something had made me feel made me clam up. I could tell him that I drove a missile into a truck and watched bodies fly, but when he asked what I was really thinking during that experience or how it made me feel . . . my mind went blank. I was nervous that if I shared the smallest emotional response, I'd immediately end up banging a drum around a fire singing

"Kum-Bay-Yah" with a bunch of teary-eyed dudes greased up with baby-oil.[12] That just wasn't going to happen.

Because I knew I had to dig deeper, though, I kept going. Over time I developed trust in David—I knew I could share painful and confusing emotions with him and he'd listen without judgement. More than that, I knew he wouldn't laugh or think less of me because I admitted being human. Eventually, David's questions helped me pull information out of hidden compartments I didn't know existed. He became my sounding board and was often the first person to hear how my experiences had made me feel. He helped me to sort through what I wanted to open up about and what should remain private, kept just between me and my very closest loved ones and confidantes. In other words, I remained in control and could still set my own limits on what I shared and what I didn't. Just because I became aware of something didn't mean I had to share it. This opening up and sorting as we went was a crucial "first step" in communicating my experiences. It gave me the confidence to share with family, friends, and, eventually, anybody who picks up the book. I couldn't have defined it at the time, but David's help with my writing was invaluable buddy-aid support for my own self-aid plan.

There aren't enough "David Hazards" to go around, though. This is where veterans' writing groups come into play. You can contact colleges, community centers, or Veterans Administration facilities and ask if they know of any veterans' writing workshops or seminars near you. Or take a look online—a quick Google search will provide links to Veterans Writing Project, Veterans Writing Group, and veterans' writing workshops all around the country. Find one that is close to you and make the effort to get

---

[12] Disturbing image courtesy of "Flash"—a Cobra pilot who served with my brother.

involved. Go to a meeting and find out if they're a good fit for you. Share with them as little or as much as you want, but, as is true with anything else, remember this:

The more you invest of yourself, the more you'll get out of it.

Mentoring, support, and a shared desire to use writing as a tool for personal growth and healing are hallmarks of these groups. If the thought of sitting behind your computer or notebook by yourself is terrifying—or mind numbingly boring—you're not alone. But don't let that derail your self-aid plan. Chances are good that the veterans in the writing group have traveled the same road you're on and they can help. More than that, they *want* to help. That's likely why they're there.

Whether you write in solitude or with guidance from a confidant, you are the only person who will know if you "got it right." If what you wrote accurately reflects what you felt—and feel—about that particular event, then you've done it right. A good way to test this is to let your narrative sit unread for several days or even a few weeks. Then reread it with fresh eyes. If what you've written doesn't trigger any "bullshit" flags, then you've succeeded. You've uncovered your compartmentalized reactions and have begun to process them.

A final step remains though—one that will carry you many steps down the road to fully returning from war.

You have to communicate your experiences to another person.

9

LOOK AT IT

By itself, reconstructing the trauma does not address the social or relational dimension of the traumatic experience. It is a necessary part of the recovery process, but it is not sufficient.

—Judith Lewis Herman, *Trauma and Recovery,*
    p.183

I HAD A GOOD FRIEND in college who loved to get hammered and expose himself in public. More than once I lost track of him while stumbling home from the bars only to find him standing proudly in the middle of the street, pants around his ankles, shouting "LOOOOOK AT IT!" to anyone within earshot. This is only tangentially connected to the focus of this chapter, and I may be rightly accused of using it as a cheap attention getter, but oh well. It's relevant because we're getting to the point in our journey where we need to share the intimate and sometimes painful information we discovered during the process of creating our own true narratives. But this doesn't mean we should hang out our junk for just anyone to see.

This chapter will explain the benefits of communicating your experiences through whatever medium works for you. I accomplished this through writing, and later, through public speaking, but those are not the only ways to do it. Want to paint yourself green and do interpretive dance in a Speedo®? Go ahead. But chances are you'll find more low-key ways to express yourself such as painting, photography, music, or drawing. Because the field of art therapy is spread across so many modes of expression, I will not attempt to introduce a comprehensive list of the different types of art here. Instead, I'll use my own experience with writing to identify the positive impact of sharing difficult information, as well as to introduce considerations for whom to share it with. What type of art should you choose? That's totally up to you. All your art needs to do is give you a way to express yourself.

But don't drop trou and "express" yourself with just anybody, not right off the bat, anyway. Your initial rounds of sharing are a continuation of the self-aid plan that started when you began recording your narrative. The information you've learned thus far in that process is intimate and deeply personal, but you probably haven't figured everything out yet. The act of sharing it with the right person will help you access the emotions and reactions that remained hidden during the creation of your narrative. But to share it without regard for the listener's *capacity and willingness to understand* risks diluting your focus at a critical point. This loss of focus will increase the odds of stagnation, of failure.

Who makes up this "trustworthy community" capable of receiving your message? They may be people close to you such as family members, good friends, or buddies you served with. Or they may be new friends you've met while engaging in healthy self-aid activities. Regardless of how long you've known them, the right person to share your narrative with is someone who can listen without judgement and is capable of sharing in your emotions. In many instances, they must be willing to go to hell with you.

The whole point of communicating the difficult emotions you uncovered in your narrative to a person you have a relationship with is that you're no longer keeping them to yourself. You're getting them outside of your head and, once released, they cannot be bottled back up. They become a known and accepted component of the relationship between you and the listener.

Drunken exposures to strangers can be denied in the light of day. Because of this escape clause, they lack the therapeutic effects of meaningful, honest sharing. But when you take the risk to truly open up to someone, neither you nor they can make it disappear again. The people you share with will know something *real* about you, and your relationship with them will deepen as a result. If you spend your life hiding behind a mask of strength, Hollywood heroism, or some shallow concept of warrior-hood, then nobody will ever truly know you. They'll only know the mask and your relationship with them will remain shallow and distant.

We, as veterans and warriors, have no further use for those masks. They are for the unproven.

SHARING: INITIALLY, IT'S ALL ABOUT SELF-AID

I'd been working on *After Action* for over a year and a half before I really understood the benefits of sharing my experiences. I'd already recorded the facts of my deployments and overlaid my emotional reactions on them through writing, but some critical connections remained missing. I found myself experiencing intense emotions but unable to tie them to specific events. This gap in my understanding was preventing me from uncovering some crucial information I knew existed but couldn't put my finger on. And it was really pissing me off.

I went internal and mulled the problem over and over in my head. For the first week or so, my wife gave me space to work it out. But eventually my distracted and distant demeanor prompted her to ask what was going on.

We sat in the quiet living room of the old farmhouse we were renting in Great Falls, Virginia. The kids were asleep upstairs, and the only noises were the wind and the dog snoring by the fireplace. Safe on the couch, I walked my wife through a battle that had occurred on the outskirts of An Numinayah during the 2003 invasion. I didn't know what I was trying to tell her, or what I was trying to figure out. I only knew that something was there and that it was bothering me. In as much detail as I could remember, I explained where we were, who was in what aircraft—she knew all my squadron mates—and each action I'd taken during the fight. Somehow, while explaining why I chose to fire and how many people I killed with each missile, I got there. I stumbled upon a hidden mental room that contained all the emotions and reactions I'd compartmentalized during the battle.

That particular battle had taken place over seven years before, but the emotions in that room hadn't aged a day. The reactions that escaped finally brought into focus what had been bothering me for all those years. They provided the connection between the person I knew I'd been before and who I was now.

For some reason, that mental room remained invisible throughout my writing process. But when I started talking through the events of that day, it became clear. I rambled on for a while, running down escaping emotions and examining them without cohesion or concern while my wife sat staring into the fire. These were the little bastards that had been thorns in my side for so long. Now that they were out in the open, there was no way I was going to let them hide again.

When it was over I sat back on the couch, drained. But contented. For the first time in years, I knew why I was upset. I knew what was making me uncomfortable. I kind of looked around the room in amazement for a moment, then looked to my wife for comment. She'd sat, unmoving and silent, for almost an hour while I talked.

Finally she spoke, "That was really hard to hear."

That wasn't the response I was expecting.

"Hard? Hard *how*?" I asked.

"I mean, I really had to focus on what you were saying to keep my mind from wandering."

This floored me. Inside I was saying, "*I'm pouring my fucking heart out and you're thinking about what? Work? A goddamn grocery list? What could have been more important?*"

Luckily, I kept my mouth shut. She continued, "It was hard to listen to because I didn't want to think about you that way—scared, angry, and hurting. I didn't want to hear that you've felt that way for years and I never knew it. I just didn't want to imagine you that way."

As hard as it was for her to hear, it did me a world of good to get it off my chest. And her reaction taught me that whomever I share with will have their own feelings and reactions to what I tell them—and they may not react the way I want, or expect. From that conversation I finally understood what had been bothering me most from my combat tours. Of equal importance was the realization that she, and the rest of my family, were not standing on the sideline. My struggles were as much theirs as mine because they were being affected by me just as I was being affected by my past. On that day I understood that I had never been alone in struggling to carry the burdens of my service.

This understanding went both ways. Now that I'd fully opened up to her, my wife understood that my random bouts of moodiness, angry flashes, and periods of withdrawal were not in response to her, the kids, or anybody else. Now that she knew they were internal fluctuations in my mood and not something that could be "fixed" by anything she could control, she was better able to help me deal with them. That one conversation gave us perspective on my experiences, strengthened our relationship, and allowed me to move forward—and she'd barely said a word. She made no attempt to explain away my emotions or try to minimize them to spare herself from sharing my pain. She just listened, regardless of how much it hurt her to do so.

Who's your "go-to" person going to be? Think about it carefully.

The person you choose to share with will play an integral role in your ability to fully understand your experiences. This person needs to understand the process you are going through and what they can do to help. One way to do this is to explain it to them. But an easier, and more thorough, approach would be to have them read this book—or at least this chapter. If you both understand the overall concept of your journey, then the chances of success are that much higher. You'll avoid recreating the wheel and the entire process can move ahead smoothly.

A NOTE TO "LISTENERS"

Asking a person to listen to the full impact of our experiences—not just the vignettes we tell at the bar—is one of the greatest honors we, as veterans, can bestow on someone. If a veteran has expressed interest in sharing with you, then take heart—you are an important person in their life. They see something that makes them believe you can understand what they've been through and that you're important enough for them to give it a shot. They are offering you a means to understand them as they are *now*—a critical bit of information if your relationship with them is to grow and progress into the future.

One of the primary things the listener needs to do is *listen*. While this may sound obvious, many of us have real difficulty listening to what someone actually says. Our mind wanders, we project our own emotions and thoughts into what's being said, and we jump ahead of the speaker by forming our own conclusions. Active listening is difficult. It takes a lot of concentration, and no small amount of self-discipline, to truly hear what someone is saying. This is especially true when the subject matter is deeply emotional—to both the speaker and the listener. It wasn't the words I said that made it hard for my wife to concentrate on our conversation. It was the pain I was revealing that made her want to seek mental shelter to protect herself.

Listeners will have to steel themselves for the uncomfortable nature of what's to come. They will also have to fight back the common tendency of trying to "fix" the problem.

Let me be perfectly clear: There is no fix to the pain caused by experiences in our past. Dead friends never come back to life. The families of those we killed will always miss them. Kids will grow up without fathers and mothers, parents will know the pain of outliving their children, and spouses will face the future without their partner and friend. Innocence lost can never be regained, and the very concept of humanity must be reevaluated after seeing what humans can do to each other. The emotions we suffer after the reality of combat are appropriate and healthy. They do not need to be "fixed." But they do need to be understood.

So, if you are the listener, don't try to fix anything—just listen. The emotions will probably come out slowly at first, but pretty soon they'll stream out under pressure. You may need to prompt and prod a little to get it going, but once the speaker accesses trapped information and begins to share it, let him or her go.

You'll know when the speaker hits this point—their knees may bounce, their eyes will become slightly unfocused in the distance or on the floor, and words will come out in compressed bursts. Raw emotions undiluted by time will pour out, very likely along with tears that may go unnoticed by the speaker. These emotions were white hot when they were compartmentalized years ago. They'll be white hot the first time they come out, too.

Silence will follow these bursts—but don't interrupt. Pauses in a normal conversation allow the other party to interject and participate. But this is not a normal conversation. These pauses are not an invitation for you to fill the silence. They are opportunities for the speaker to find the right words to describe something he or she has never said before—or maybe didn't even realize could be said. This is about *them*, not you, and they must remain firmly focused on the particulars of their experiences, not anyone else's. There will be time to share your insights later but for right now, just listen. The accumulated pus of trapped emotions must be allowed to spew out unhindered.

BUDDY AID: THE BUILT-IN COMMUNITY

> What a returning soldier needs most when leaving war is not a mental health professional but a living community to whom his experience matters. There is usually such a community close at hand: his or her surviving comrades.
>
> —Jonathan Shay, *Achilles in Vietnam*, p.198

The listener who provides your buddy-aid doesn't have to be a family member. Nor do you have to rely on only one person. At various times throughout my journey, I have relied on my brother, sister, father, and mother to help me understand things I was having trouble with. I've also used long runs with a close combat buddy to chew on reactions that I was having a hard time processing. And of course, my wife—a veteran herself—helps immensely as well. My relationships with each of these people are different and so is the support I gain from sharing with them.

But what if your relationships with friends and family don't support this kind of sharing? Then it's time to call in some buddy-aid.

Remember the young Marine who almost killed the boy while on patrol in Ramadi? He's a prime example of someone who didn't feel comfortable sharing with friends and family—or even his VA counselor. Even though he'd asked for corpsman-aid, it just didn't work for him. He just couldn't open up and tell anyone about the boy he'd almost killed. Luckily, buddy-aid was available.

For him, buddy aid came in the form of Semper Fi Odyssey, a week-long retreat designed to assist wounded veterans transition out of the service. Created and run by retired Major General T.S. Jones, Semper Fi Odyssey helps wounded veterans develop realistic plans for their future after they leave the service. The nonreligious, week-long program of instruction focuses on defining and understanding the four fundamental components of a whole, healthy person: Mental, Emotional, Physical, and Spiritual.

General Jones brings team leaders—most of whom are combat veterans from Iraq, Afghanistan, or Vietnam—and wounded veterans to a secluded camp in the hills of central Pennsylvania. Internet and cell coverage are spotty at best, and the isolation of the camp creates the opportunity for introspective thought and honest self-evaluation. The atmosphere of the camp—unconditional positive regard and a sense of shared profound experiences—is almost as crucial to the participants' success as the actual instruction.

It was at this camp that the young sergeant finally shared what had been bothering him. I happened to be the one he shared with, but it could have been any of us. It wasn't the friends he'd buried, nor the Iraqis he'd killed that were haunting him. It was the decision he'd made while staring at the boy with the rifle. His conscious decision to kill the boy was in direct conflict with his self-image as a good, caring person. The fact that the boy lived didn't matter in the least. He'd made the decision to kill him— and now he knew what he was capable of.

His immediate, violent reaction to his son jumping on his back put him right back behind the .50cal. The years between the events evaporated in a heartbeat, and he saw himself clearly capable of hurting a child—this time his own. The belief that he posed a very real, lethal threat to his own family reinforced his willingness to do anything possible to keep them safe. Including removing himself from their lives. He'd contemplated doing it permanently—the guns were all in his room in the house—but hadn't. Not yet.

He told me all this through a series of explosive bursts of conversation. I sat quietly during the interludes as his tears dropped unnoticed on the head of his therapy dog. When I sensed he needed a break, or a chance to regroup, I shared some of my experiences. I never offered platitudes or promised that he'd be okay. I didn't need to. The effect of just telling another person these deeply painful emotions seemed to lift a weight from his chest. The words he spoke carried poisons from deep within and, as they poured out, his personality emerged from hiding. Over the course of the next hour, small inflections of voice, self-deprecating jokes, and how he wiped tears off on his shoulder with a look that said, "well shit, this sucks," all told me that the real man inside—not the tortured, self-hating soul—was coming back.

He knew that he had a long way to go still. He knew that counseling offered the best chance for him to fully heal and, now that he knew he was neither alone nor weak, he was willing to give the VA another chance—this time without withholding critical information from his counselor.

He was, and is, a proud man to whom the very idea of admitting pain goes against his concept of strength. But his concept of strength matured when he realized his family *needed* him in their lives. They stood to lose a father and husband if he didn't step up and face his demons. Barricading himself in the back bedroom suddenly felt like cowardice—and he was no coward.

We don't keep in touch anymore, although I'd love to hear from him again. Our conversation, sitting on a rock wall at a camp in central Pennsylvania, served its purpose. The atmosphere created by General Jones set the stage for this Marine to achieve in a single, transformative conversation what had taken me several years of writing to do for myself. He realized why he was upset, knew he was not alone, and knew he was not a monster. More importantly, he knew if he dedicated himself to healing, then he had a bright future *with* the family he loves—not isolated and forever quarantined for their protection.

This is buddy-aid at its finest. If you don't know where else to start—or find yourself slipping back into stagnation—contact Semper Fi Odyssey. Or any other, similar nonprofit for that matter. They exist because caring, compassionate people, many of whom are veterans themselves, have figured out their own paths home and want to share what they've learned along the way.

None of us faced the challenges of combat alone. There's no reason to face the challenges of coming home alone, either.

10

"DOC!"

BY THIS POINT IN MY JOURNEY, I figured I had it all under control. My self-aid consisted of spearfishing and free-diving to quiet the physical aftereffects of combat and writing to understand the emotional ones. I had developed my self-awareness to the point where I was able to understand the genesis of my emotions and reactions significantly better than before. I felt I had successfully moved past my combat experiences and had really, finally, come home.

But I hadn't. Unresolved aspects of my combat experiences lingered deep beneath my well-adjusted exterior. I'd handled the physical and emotional issues pretty well. But now—ten years after coming home from Iraq—I finally realized I needed help with the spiritual ones.

It was a hard step because I took a lot of pride in the idea that I'd been able to handle everything myself. I'd spent three years processing, reconstructing, and recording my emotions and reactions to combat and was confident I'd figured them out. Hell, I'd written a book that other veterans said had helped *them*. I'd even provided buddy-aid for other veterans at Semper Fi Odyssey—and had been good at it! I took all that as evidence that I was golden, that I had healed myself and was moving forward on my own.

I was so certain that I'd taken care of all the aftereffects of combat that when I began to feel depressed I knew there had to be a different reason. At the time we were living in suburban northern Virginia and, while the area had a certain beauty, I'd never felt truly comfortable there. It was too manicured, too hemmed in by urban sprawl, and the lifestyle there just didn't work for me. But I told myself it was temporary and that we'd move again soon. Only "soon" kept moving farther into the future. When a couple of years stretched into three, with no end in sight, I tried to stop thinking about moving on. Instead I focused all my attention on raising our two kids.

Raising our kids. That was a worthy place to sink my energy and effort. I learned a lot about parenting from my own parents. Their examples form the baseline for how I do, and do not, want to interact with my own children. As with many facets of my life, my father is my prime role model. He's a great dad, but he wasn't perfect. Growing up, Dad set rules that were to be followed to the letter. If they were broken, he could flash to white-hot anger in what seemed like a heartbeat. As a young boy this reaction scared and threatened me and, when my infant son came home from the hospital, I promised myself I wouldn't act the same way. But I had inherited Dad's temper, and the challenges of parenting seemed custom-made to test my restraint.

It was my failure to control this temper that brought unease and self-loathing back into my life. Amid the shade of oak trees and scent of jasmine in Virginia, the emotions I thought I had processed out of my system by writing *After Action* came back to haunt me. Only they seemed a little darker than before, like they could erase any happy thought and make my whole outlook on life change for the worse. I couldn't put a finger on the exact cause—but there was a pattern to when this darkness hit me the hardest.

It always started with a blowup. The kids would catch me when I was tired, frustrated, or trying to get something accomplished. They'd whine, willfully cross any line I told them not to, and generally exert their two- and four-year-old senses of independence by obstructing every effort I made to complete the day's tasks.

And then I'd lose my temper.

Red-faced and screaming, I would bowl them over with righteous daddy-anger. My voice would deepen in timber and gain the harshness of threatened violence. Even as I felt this dangerous anger rise, I could do nothing to stop it. When it erupted I could hear my father's voice echoing in my head—and knew the impact it was having on the scared, immediately penitent, four-year-old boy in front of me. It was a sour victory, a bully's victory. Worse, I'd failed in my primary goal of killing the anger. It remained as strong as ever.

In the aftermath of these blowups, I'd get depressed. The only solid goal I'd set for myself as a father and I had just failed at it. Again. Not only that, but the growing suspicion that writing *After Action* hadn't been the final act in my return, that I hadn't succeeded in moving on to "happily-ever-after" was making me feel like a charlatan, a faker. Even the book reviews and emails from other veterans thanking me for helping them made me feel like a failure. They were just being nice, I told myself. How could I have helped them when I hadn't helped myself?

The periods of darkness lasted anywhere from a few days to a few weeks. Sometimes they grouped together into longer stretches. It seemed that as soon as I came out of one slump, the kids would get my goat again—and down I'd go. I was stuck in this cycle and dimly aware of my own role in perpetuating it. But I didn't know how to break it.

THE CONFRONTATION

I've always sucked at acting happy when I'm not. Lena, my wife, finally grew tired of my continued professions that everything was "fine" and confronted me one evening after dinner. We were walking through Reston Town Center, a group of high-rises, restaurants, and shops built to look like city blocks—manicured Disney World versions of city blocks—amid the suburban sprawl outside of Washington, DC. The cold December wind raced through the gaps in the buildings and straight through our thin jackets. Hands jammed in our pockets, we kept walking around the block, talking in the carefully considered words of a conversation where everything is on the table.

She knew I was unhappy, really unhappy, but I couldn't tell her why. I felt silly admitting that my inability to control my anger was causing me such distress. I wanted a solution to the problem but didn't know what it was. She offered up possibilities I was too chicken to voice.

"Is it me you're unhappy with? Our marriage?"

"No."

"Then what—watching the kids? Are you unhappy staying home?"

"No, it's not that. All I know is that I can't stay here—in this place. It's not you, it's not the kids; I just can't stay here." That was it—I grabbed onto that thought like a lifeline.

"I just hate this place." There, I said it.

Whatever it was that was boiling up inside me had to be Virginia's fault. If I could just get back to California, back to the escape offered by the Pacific Ocean, then everything would be all right. The cold waters near our house in San Diego had given me the means to quell the unease and irritability before. Maybe that was all I needed to control the anger once and for all. If we could just get back there, I'd beat it. That was it. I needed the ocean, the release it offered, to be happy. Anything less would just not work.

This was not news to Lena. We'd always talked about returning to San Diego someday. She just didn't realize that my "someday" couldn't wait until after retirement. She agreed that we should move back but with one caveat. If moving back to California didn't take care of whatever was bothering me, then I needed to get professional help. I readily agreed. After all, I was sure a change of venue was all I needed. I'd be fine once I could dissipate the energy myself.

It took a little finagling, but six months after our shivering conversation, we moved back to California.

At first it seemed to do the trick. We moved back into our old house, hit our old haunts again, got the kids boogie boards and snorkel kits, and spent hours on the beach. San Diego was everything we remembered and more. It truly felt like we were home.

YOU CAN RUN BUT YOU CAN'T HIDE

But after the dust settled from our move, the darkness came back. I didn't even have to fully lose my temper with the kids to feel like I was losing my battle to be a good dad. Just feeling the anger rise in me was enough. Even with the outlets of surfing and diving, the tension didn't go away. One day I found myself staring over the deep blue waters of the Pacific from a bluff, depressed, angry, and out of ideas. The car was loaded in the parking lot with a surfboard and all my spearfishing gear—but I was too distracted and depressed to feel like using them. I'd fired my last round and it hadn't killed the beast. It was then, when I realized that even amongst the natural beauty I'd pined over for years I remained unhappy, that I knew I had to ask for help.

Right. Help. But where?

My perception of the Veterans Administration was not a good one. I'd only gone to one VA facility when I first left active duty and swore I'd never go back. The entire building reeked of stress and bureaucratic roadblocks. Every office had lines of greying veterans sitting outside it, waiting their turn to have their complaint heard. Just walking in the door made me feel uncomfortable, like I was going to catch something contagious. I'd dropped off my paperwork as quickly as possible and left, vowing never to return.

I really wasn't interested in going to the VA. I feared that, if I did somehow get an appointment, they'd write me a prescription and send me on my way. Or that I'd spend three hours with some civilian counselor trying to explain what a "Marine" is. How was someone like that supposed to understand me enough to be able to help? And I sure as hell didn't want to resort to using drugs. Realizing I needed help was one thing. But figuring out *who* to talk to was another. Then a friend recommended I look into the local Vet Center.

Tentatively, I called the number for the San Marcos Vet Center. On the second ring it was answered by a young voice, crisp and clear, as if answering the battalion duty phone. Within minutes I was speaking with a counselor. He gave me the rundown of what the Vet Center offered and asked if I wanted to come in immediately—or if I could wait until Thursday morning. He explained that was when they did routine orientation interviews for veterans new to the Center.

I went in the next Thursday—and all my fears proved to be groundless. It wasn't in a huge building designed to house every possible function of the VA under one confusing roof. The Vet Center occupies a suite of offices in the San Marcos City Hall.

Want to feel welcome and comfortable walking into a building? Then go to San Marcos City Hall. You walk on shaded paths past babbling fountains to get to the main entrance. Three-story glass windows fill the lobby with light and a smiling receptionist greets you as you come in. The cool air is quiet and calm and you wonder if caffeine is even allowed in the building—or just herbal tea. A display case features the huge painting of a bearded veteran leaning against the Vietnam Memorial Wall, as his fallen comrades press their hands against his from within. The door to the Vet Center is prominently marked and I actually felt proud that I belonged there. This is not a place where veterans slink in quietly. It is a place where pride of service is evident, and respect for our sacrifices is freely given.

Entering the suite you're immediately greeted by the receptionist. A cheerful welcome, please sign in, and can I get you a cup of coffee? Where were the sullen gate guards I'd feared? Where were the piles of red tape I had to deal with? Shouldn't I be overhearing someone complaining loudly about *something* by now? It was too efficient, too welcoming, and too comfortable to be true. There had to be a catch. Maybe I'd find it when—if—I finally got to see a counselor. Probably some psychologist who couldn't get a job elsewhere, sucking on the government tit. Yup, I figured, that must be it—that's where this Vet Center charade will fall apart.

The first counselor I spoke with had been a Marine amtrac[13] driver. He'd spent two deployments in Iraq in an infantry role, and my fears of having to do hours of elementary explanations evaporated. After we shared basic histories, he explained what the Vet Center does, who can use its services, and what the normal

---

[13] Contraction of amphibious tractor, nickname of the AAV-7 Amphibious Assault Vehicle.

flow of counseling looks like. The Vet Center program began in the 1970s and has grown to over 300 locations across the United States. Technically part of the Veterans Administration, Vet Centers are specially designed and staffed to focus on the needs of combat veterans, their families, and victims of military sexual trauma.

GOING IN

The next Thursday I met with the counselor assigned to me. Appropriately enough, he'd been a corpsman in his earlier career. A retired Senior Chief, Michael[14] had spent most of his naval service on the "green side," tending to wounded Marines. He is a soft-spoken bear of a man with a slight Jamaican accent, and he immediately made me feel at home. I saw him once a week for a month or so, then once a month after that. In a very short period of time, Michael was able to help me identify what was bothering me, figure out a way to mitigate it, and erase the depressive cycle that had followed me from Virginia to California.

Nothing magical took place in Michael's office. He didn't lift any curses from my soul or prescribe drugs that would rewire my brain. All he did was listen—and apply his clinical knowledge of combat trauma to the specifics of my experiences. I played a role in the positive outcome as well. The extensive program of self-aid I'd undertaken had set me up well for quick, effective counseling.

He didn't have to sift through years of memories to get to the root cause of what was bothering me. Neither did I try and hide anything or stubbornly refuse to share difficult emotions or memories. I basically dumped the entirety of my experiences on his desk and said, "Here it is—help me figure it out."

And he did.

---

[14] Not his real name.

GETTING TO THE ROOT

What was it that was bothering me? What was upsetting me so much that it could erase all the positive aspects of my life and leave me depressed and angry? It all boiled down to one thing— one simple statement that formed what I'd thought was a healthy perspective on my combat experiences. It was supposed to free me from the guilt I'd brought home from combat. Instead, it just gave the guilt a sheltered room in which to grow.

In the final stages of writing *After Action,* I'd uncovered the root cause of my unease. It had been the killing of other human beings that bothered me most about Iraq. The act of killing called into question my very self-identity as a good person and, as a result, made me question whether I was worthy of anything happy or good in life. Sure, they'd been enemy soldiers and I was just doing my job, but they'd still been people. What's done is done, however, and I couldn't bring them back to life. I decided that this was my burden to bear, the fact that I'd killed people, and I just had to figure out a way to move forward in life carrying it.

I did that by wrapping it all up in one succinct phrase—the phrase that was supposed to shrink my burden but ended up engorging it.

Good people don't kill. I killed. What does that make me?

I meant it as a way to remind myself to always do good. But this phrase, and the burden it describes, became my "stuck point." In PTSD, a stuck point is a place where rational thought breaks down. The mind ceases to process information or reach conclusions based on solid, rational thinking. Instead, it leaps ahead to a manufactured, foregone conclusion that is usually not supported by the facts. That's what this phrase was doing to me. Let me explain.

By concretely separating what a "good" person does from what a "bad" person does, I'd created a division in my own spiritual landscape. I'd set up a big "compartment," if you will, into which I sent all the memories and feelings about what I'd done that was "bad." This had nothing to do with religion, and everything to do with the morals and ethics I brought with me into the service. That they resonated perfectly with the core values espoused by the Marine Corps reinforced them to the point where they became nearly impenetrable.

And the problem with this "good/bad" spiritual landscape was that it left no room for phrases like *"Good people don't kill,"* to be interpreted in any other way than simple black and white. It left no room for the gray areas that always, naturally arise in the theater of war.

As a result, there was no way to answer the hanging statement and question—*I killed. What does that make me?*—without self-identifying as a bad person. The guiding force in my life, therefore, became atoning for the fact that I had killed other human beings. But I felt like my balance sheet was so far in the negative that each small failure weighed much more than any good thing I could possibly do. My own self-image became that of a fundamentally bad person.

How does this factor into the depression that followed me from Virginia? The answer is, the same way the young sergeant's guilt at deciding to kill the Iraqi boy poisoned his relationship with his own son.

Every time I failed to control my temper, my mind raced ahead to my stuck point. I didn't allow reality with all its gray areas to factor in. It didn't matter that sometimes kids need to see an angry response when they misbehave, or that getting mad is a normal human reaction that needs to be expressed. Instead,

I took every loss of composure—even small ones that the kids didn't even notice—as reinforcement of my self-image as a fundamentally bad person.

The logic loop went like this: *I swore to not shout at my kids—I shouted at my kids—I killed people and I'm a bad person—I swore to not shout at my kids—I shouted at my kids—I killed people and I'm a bad* . . . And it would continue, unbroken. It sounds silly now, but at the time that loop made me believe I deserved no happiness in my life, that because of my actions in combat, suffering was the only future I deserved. But I couldn't see it myself. It wasn't until Michael showed me the loop that I recognized its existence.

When I explained to Michael what bothered me most about Iraq, he immediately zeroed in on the phrase, "*Good people don't kill. I killed. What does that make me?*" He explained what a stuck point is and asked me if I thought that phrase was mine. It obviously was, but he let me mull it over for a few minutes in silence.

That small application of good listening skills, coupled with his clinical knowledge, exposed the ultimate reason why I'd been feeling depressed. I consider myself a pretty self-aware individual, and I've spent a lot of time contemplating my experiences and reactions to them, but I still needed someone else to help me understand the spiritual impact of my experiences.

Michael didn't stop there. Identifying the stuck point is one thing, but in order to remove its ability to shortcut rational thought it needed to be removed from the loop. Again, there were no magic words spoken, no incense or chanting filling the air. Sitting in his quiet office, Michael simply asked me if there was any other way to word that phrase—maybe a way that didn't presuppose the answer.

I balked at the suggestion. Actually, when Michael opened his mouth to speak I immediately got angry. It welled up from somewhere deep inside and I just barely kept it hidden. The memory of the last time I had engaged in a conversation on this subject, in a chapel tent in the Kuwaiti desert, had popped unexpectedly into my head.

THE CHAPLAIN

It was about a week after the invasion of Iraq and I'd stopped into the chapel after my mission for that night had been cancelled. Something had been bothering me and I finally decided to ask the chaplain a question. I wanted to know how God felt about us killing other human beings. Truth be told, I just wanted the chaplain to magically make me feel better about whacking Iraqi soldiers with rockets and missiles.

He didn't. Instead, the chaplain responded with a recital of how badly Saddam Hussein treated his own people, how he killed and imprisoned them indiscriminately, and how his actions made him an evil man. Guess he missed "how to avoid making bad comparisons" day in chaplain school. Then he asked if I thought we were doing the right thing by removing Saddam from power, as if I'd just been too simple-minded to see how two wrongs *obviously* make a right.

I left that tent angrier than I'd ever been in my life. That man, and probably my own naive expectations of what he could do, had made me feel stupid, ashamed, and weak—pretty much the trifecta of shitty feelings for any warrior. Stumbling into the blackness of the Kuwaiti night, I swore to bury those thoughts and questions deeply. They were never going to come out again; I'd see to that.

Yet there I was, sitting in Michael's quiet office, asking essentially the same question ten years later, "Am I a bad person?" When I realized the parallels between my failed attempt to get spiritual guidance from the chaplain and my current attempt to get secular spiritual help from my counselor, I braced myself for another disappointment.

I didn't think something so simple as muttering a few words would make any difference. I didn't know what would erase my stuck point, but it sure as hell wouldn't be quick or easy. This thing was so deeply entrenched it was messing with the core of my being. I knew I would have to work hard and long to dig it out.

I was wrong.

In his quiet Jamaican accent, Michael simply asked, "When do good people kill?"

His words shot straight into my soul. Because of the years of self-assessment and dedicated attempts to truly understand the impact of my experiences, I could see the value of those words as soon as he spoke them. They replaced the shaming, damning, self-hating phrase that had derailed my healing process. They correctly described my situation by allowing that sometimes good people *must* do bad things. No longer was I to be forever reminded that I was a bad person because I killed. Those words did not erase the fact that I'd killed—nothing could do that— but they gave me a healthy way to look at myself in light of my actions in combat.

The phrase is still the burden I bear—it remains my personal burden of peace—and I *want* to remember it. It is the essence of my warrior experience and will forever remind me of the sacrifices I, and millions of others, made in service of our country.

But the burden is now a productive thing, a reminder to do good whenever possible without automatic condemnation for the actions of my past.

MORE GOOD TO COME

I've figured out a lot about my reactions to combat on my own. But it took a calm, quiet professional to help me defuse the spiritual reactions that threatened to roll back all my advances. I was unable to apply self- and buddy-aid to the spiritual aftereffects of combat because I didn't understand that they existed. Luckily, I found a corpsman at the right time and place.

It took moving to California and an ultimatum from my wife for me to finally seek, and accept, professional help. In other words, it took a lot. Unfortunately, many veterans wait until something catastrophic happens before talking to someone. We recoil from anything remotely selfish and, to a warrior's way of thinking, devoting time to one's personal issues at the perceived expense of others is a selfish act.

But as you'll see in the next section, facing these internal challenges is about as unselfish as you can get.

PART THREE:

DUTY

11

AS UNSELFISH
AS IT GETS

"Cover me, I'm fucked!"
"Fuck you—I'm covered!"

*—Conversation between two grunts at Thermopylae,
Fallujah, and every battle in-between*

IT DOESN'T MATTER if you're a grunt, an admin clerk, motor transport, or a high-speed, low-drag recon guy, there's somebody in your unit who's a selfish prick. This guy—or gal—always makes sure they're taken care of first. Their pay is never screwed up, their vehicle always has the chow and water in it, their shelter is always the first one up and comfortable, and they never lift a finger to help anybody else.

Selfishness, as much as we act like it doesn't occur in the military, is an unavoidable attribute of humans everywhere. At some point, the unselfish majority of service members realize they cannot change the selfish ones and quit trying. Instead, they double-down on their own selflessness in an attempt to make up for those who are only looking out for themselves. They become almost violently selfless—aggressively seeking any opportunity to put the needs of others first. To the veterans who fall into this category, and it is the majority of us, everything I've written thus far has likely sounded selfish.

As well it should. Because up to now the continuing actions described in this book have required veterans to go internal, to focus all their effort and energy on overcoming their *own* challenges. As I showed with examples from my own life, this requires taking time away from family, work, studies, and making money in order to get your own physical, mental, and spiritual house in order. This sounds like the very definition of selfish.

But it's not.

IT'S NOT SELFISH BECAUSE OF WHAT COMES NEXT

Nobody gets a medal for completing their journey. There's no secret handshake, no plaque to hang on the wall, and no elevated social status for achieving it. The last-place runner in a 5k gets more overt congratulations for their efforts than you will. But that's never been the point of this journey. The warrior's journey is one of discovery, not for our own gain, but so we can help others.

Just as helping a comrade in battle is part of our duty, so is helping a comrade at home. Executing this duty, however, is not as straightforward as just dragging them out of the line of fire. For the vast majority of us, the knowledge and skills required to assist others through the challenges of coming home are not innate. They must be learned.

Returning warriors must initially focus on their own challenges because that is the only way to attain the tools they'll need to help others. You have to experience the confusion, loss of purpose and maybe your faith, and also the deep betrayal of having your emotions seemingly turn against you—*and then learn to deal with these issues*—before you can help somebody else do the same.

Overcoming the personal challenges of the first three phases of the warrior's return—physical, emotional, and spiritual—were the prerequisites to reach this point. Your efforts up till now *had* to be directed inward. From this point on, however, they go outward. This is the final phase of the warrior's return—the one where we share what we've learned to help others. To invest blood, sweat, and tears into extracting something valuable from your experiences, and then share it freely with those who need it the most, is the very opposite of selfish.

FINDING THE BOON

Love it or hate it, your time in the service has put you through experiences that have given you something, something valuable that is hard to put into words. Like the archetypal warriors in mythology, your journey has transformed you. You've learned things few others have, changed, and emerged from the crucible of service as a different person. It is in the essence of this personal transformation that we find what Campbell described as "the boon."

The mythological warrior's journey doesn't end until he or she returns from the unknown bearing something of value. This "thing" is most often enhanced consciousness, a changed worldview, or something beneficial to the warrior's community as a whole. Gaining this boon, and returning to share it with others, is the whole point of the warrior's journey. It's what elevates the journey beyond just a series of adventures.

The definition of what could be considered a boon has changed with time. Back when a warrior's skill on the battlefield decided life or death for the entire community, the boon may have been victory itself. World Wars I and II may have had this aspect due to the immensity of the conflicts, but few other modern wars attain that level of existential threat. Negotiated settlements, political interests, and laws of armed conflict have removed total annihilation of the losing side as a true possibility in modern combat. More often than not, wars are now fought to achieve limited goals and objectives. Individual warrior's efforts to secure victory achieve little notice in the community because the community as a whole has very little at stake.

So what boon can the modern warrior offer society? If fire has already been brought down from the gods, technology and

science have proven what our world is and isn't, and worldviews
are formed by instant media access to the farthest reaches of the
planet, then what of value is left for the warrior to bring back
from the unknown?

Wisdom and insight.

The wisdom and insight gained by experience, by thought-
ful consideration, and by becoming conscious of what is truly
important in life. These are the modern warrior's boon. The
terrible trials and ordeals of combat, if survived, offer warriors
unique opportunities to learn and grow. These opportunities are
not for the faint of heart and, indeed, to experience them we
must spend time at the fragile border between life and death.
But the warrior who has seen, done, and survived the arena of
combat has earned the opportunity to learn valuable lessons. The
boon of wisdom is theirs for the taking.

To do this, though, to achieve the wisdom and maturity of
experience that is the veteran's boon to society, returning warriors
must overcome the challenges of their return. The physical, emotional, and spiritual impacts of combat must be acknowledged,
understood, and incorporated into our identity and awareness.
Only by refusing to stagnate and choosing to complete our
journey can we gain the wisdom of our experiences.

Then we can look for the opportunity to share it—and fulfill
our duty to our comrades in the process.

THE COMMUNITY

To whom do we offer our hard-earned wisdom and maturity? As
loudly as America's love for her veterans is proclaimed in adver-
tisements and media reports, the population as a whole is not
waiting with baited breath for our wisdom to pour forth. Before
that can happen we, veterans as a whole, must demonstrate the

value of our wisdom. And for most veterans this will not occur at the national level. We may end up there, but first we must look closer to home to find the community most willing and able to benefit from the boon we've wrested from our adventures.

FAMILY

The people closest to us form the core of our community. Our family members, especially our kids, bear the brunt of our burdens if we stagnate. Physical isolation, emotional coldness, flashes of rage, and unpredictable responses are how we transfer our burdens on to them. But if we do the hard work required to push through the challenges of our return, they stand to benefit the most.

Buddha is credited with the insightful phrase, "Life is suffering." Well, he had a point. Look around you. The reality is that everyone you know will die. The ability to ignore this fact is one of the first luxuries combat takes away from us. We've seen how fragile the human body is, how a huge personality bleeds into the dirt just the same as a meek one. Our relationship with death is one of equanimity and respect; we can respect its inevitability while refusing to make its job any easier.

Our family members are unlikely to have this same understanding. During times of family grief or tragedy, they will be confronted by the uncomfortable truths of life, often when they are least prepared to deal with them. During these times of crisis, the wisdom we've extracted from our experiences can be most valuable. We can be the pillar they lean on for support. A word, a touch, a look that lets them know we understand their pain, without them having to explain it, can make all the difference to someone imagining they are alone. It's not that we can fix what has happened, but rather our ability to understand their pain that makes our support unique and effective.

And it's not only in the arena of death and suffering where our wisdom has value. The ability to pass on life lessons, guide others through difficult transitions, and provide a solid foundation for our children to develop into responsible adults are also part of the returning warrior's boon. Combat is a savage but effective teacher. The life lessons we learned under fire, the struggles of transitioning into, and out of, the military, and the awareness we gained by unpacking our reactions to combat have matured us beyond our years. The life wisdom born of this maturity is the boon that can provide calm and steady guidance through any challenges we, or our families, face in the future.

OTHER VETERANS

Regardless whether you are an orphan or are surrounded by multiple generations of your kin, another community exists that stands to benefit from the efforts you make to find your boon—veterans.

Every warrior will need to figure out their own way to transition home. But that doesn't mean we can't help each other do it. For every veteran who overcomes the challenges of coming home, there are many more who've stagnated. You know them. They are our brothers and sisters who can't move on, who are mired in rage and hate. They are the ones who hide behind HESCO barriers filled with misconceptions and refuse to patrol. They are not living in the present, only dying in the past.

They cannot be goaded into leaving their imagined security. Encouraging them to honestly examine their emotions elicits angry responses and accusations of weakness. They regularly retreat behind social media avatars and spew hatred and rage online, portraying themselves as living reincarnations of the

Spartan 300—stoic defenders of a population they denigrate for requiring protection while simultaneously longing to feel part of it. Far from the physical battlefields where they fought, these men and women maintain their combat mindset as if their life still depends on it. It is fear of the work required to heal their inner wounds and reestablish their concept of humanity that is keeping them from moving forward. In their never-ending battle, the threats they protect against are no longer external. They're internal.

How can we, their brothers- and sisters-in-arms, help them recognize this? How can we overcome the anger and scorn they direct at us when we attempt to pull back the curtain on their suffering? There is a way we can do this that doesn't involve confrontation. It requires leadership that encourages without ultimatums, that empowers rather than subordinates the follower, and that fosters initiative on all levels. It's called "leadership by example" and it is the foundational ethos of any good leader.

Imagine a platoon in full MOPP[15] gear, gas masks and all. Dead birds and dogs give evidence that it was not a drill, that deadly gas really was used. When the "All Clear" sounds, there is no mad rush to strip off the protective gear. Foul-smelling gas masks remain tight against their faces as they cast nervous glances at each other. But they can't stay like that forever. The platoon has work to do, a mission to accomplish. They cannot stagnate in fear. Eventually someone takes the risk. He breaks the seal on his mask and the rest of the platoon watches closely.

First breath. Is he going to die?

No coughing, no tears. Maybe a fake grimace if he's a joker,

---

[15] Mission Oriented Protective Posture: gas masks, gloves, boots, and special suits designed to protect the wearer from nuclear, chemical, and biological agents.

then a smile. Everybody strips off their masks and inhales deeply. When they exhale, their tension goes, too.

This is the situation our modern warrior's journey leaves us in. We all return home wearing the gas mask of compartmentalization. Then we retreat into our holes, houses, and communities and struggle to breathe. The "All Clear" sounds a thousand times but cannot reach our ears. It's not until we see someone else, someone like us, take their mask off—and live—that we grow strong enough to do it, too.

RETURNING TO A FULL, RICH LIFE

The compartmented life is a half-life, with emotions blunted and separated from conscious thoughts and actions. We want to be that perfect dad, mom, son, or daughter. We want our lovers to know us inside and out—our weaknesses as well as our strengths. We want to develop nurturing relationships with our children and for them to know we love them more than life itself. But we can't live a life like that if we choose to keep our masks on.

We fool ourselves into believing our bullying and strict discipline are intended to make ourselves and our kids tougher, better equipped to handle life's challenges. We may even see living an emotional half-life as some sick badge of honor and accept it as an unavoidable part of being a warrior. Much of our concept of strength revolves around the falsehood that, to be strong, you must control and suppress any emotional response not reeking of testosterone. As wrong as this sentiment is, it is an aspect of American culture that veterans may have to address before they can gain the courage to break the seal.

When General Patton got in trouble for slapping a shell-shocked soldier who was in a hospital in Italy, he explained that he was trying to motivate the young man to shake it off, to buck up. While a physical act like that is unthinkable today, there are still people in our society who believe veterans suffering PTSD and postservice adjustment issues are whiny babies who just need to "man up."

This is the message of ignorance.

Whether ill-considered or criminally stupid, people who make statements that our veterans are somehow weak for experiencing normal human emotions are saying that our military consists of disposable heroes. They're promoting the simple-minded concept that the only benefit a warrior has to society is on the battlefield, and usually by dying there. They don't seem to realize that our nation stands to benefit tremendously from an influx of well-adjusted veterans empowered by the conscious wisdom of their experiences. The only way to gain that wisdom is to fully expose ourselves to the traumas of our past.

If these individuals are veterans, I recommend they take an honest look at themselves and consider how damaging their statements are to their brothers and sisters who *have* shown the courage to face their demons. Those who make these statements without having served should be ignored as fools. While we fought to protect their right of free speech, among other things, that doesn't mean we have to listen to their message of ignorance that serves to enslave and marginalize us.

Veterans do not have to bury their emotions forever. We do not have to meekly accept that our service will always force us to react in ways we know to be hurtful to our, and our families', happiness. We are warriors, not victims, and we have a choice to make: Stagnate in fear or advance to face our challenges head-on. Attacking and overcoming our obstacles is the only real option.

But somebody has to be first to go over the wall, somebody

has to be first to take off their gas mask. Your buddies from combat are waiting for you to break the seal, to begin the process of de-compartmentalization. You can lead from the front and *show*, rather than tell, them how to move forward. And by taking the initiative to address your own challenges of coming home, you are leading by example for the entire veteran community, not just your close buddies.

OH, AND ANOTHER THING . . .

If the thought of investing serious time and energy in your own health and happiness still makes you feel selfish, here's another consideration. The two primary beneficiaries of the wisdom you stand to gain if you *do* focus on yourself for a bit—your family and other veterans—may very well be one and the same.

According to a recent survey conducted by the Pew Research Center, veterans are more likely than members of the general public to have family connections to the military. Seventy-nine percent of veterans surveyed had immediate family members who also served, as opposed to 61% of the general public. This gap grows larger among respondents under 40 years of age—60% of these veterans had an immediate family member who also served as opposed to 39% of the general public.

While interesting, the concentration of volunteers among families with a strong tradition of military service may not be enough to push a stubborn and proud veteran to face the challenges of coming home. They may imagine their grandfather never had any problems after WWII, so why should they have any after Iraq? Even if in their hearts they know this to be false, family myths and legends are difficult to overcome. This is why, in light of the following trend, it is more important than ever for today's veterans to face the challenges of coming home openly, honestly, and without considering themselves selfish or weak for doing so:

> The biggest gap in terms of family connections is in the share [of the population] that has a child who has served in the military. Veterans are more than twice as likely as members of the general public to say they have a son or daughter who has served. (The Military-Civilian Gap: Fewer Family Connections, 23 November 2011 by Kim Parker www.pewsocialtrends.org)

This report tells us there is more than double the chance that your kid(s)—if you have any—will choose to serve *because you did*. If this doesn't reach in and grab hold of your parental responsibility bone, then nothing will. There may be nothing you can do to influence your child's decision to serve—rail against the military and they may rebel against you, encourage it as their duty and they may rebel against you. Regardless of your opinions of military service, your children will know that you served and that your period of service had a profound impact on you. Their model of what it means to be a mature adult will include some aspect of military service in it. That's just the way it works.

They may serve, they may not. But if they do, then they will likely face the same trials and challenges you faced. Indeed, that may be their primary motivation to serve—to prove that they can fight the same battles as you did. The military will prepare them very well to go into combat. But the leftover physical reactions, the chasm between their conscious and unconscious minds, and the shattered remains of their humanity are all going to follow them home from their battlefields, just like they did for us. It is unlikely that military culture will adapt quickly enough to address these issues in time to help our kids. But we can.

It is our responsibility to prepare our children for the challenges of coming home. Don't have any? Nieces, nephews, and other young people in your community count as well. The challenges they will face, should they choose to serve, have not changed for thousands of years. They'll face them because they want to test their mettle, and they'll discover, just as we did, that the transformation they seek comes at a cost.

These young people will need role models, mentors, and heroes to show them how to handle that cost. What kind will you be? One who hides the truth and rearms the trap of stagnation? Or one with the strength to face, deal with, and share the full truth of what war does to human beings?

If you wish to feed the boon of your knowledge back into the loop, I encourage you to use this book as the starting point for the return phase of your own journey. Armed with the background information in the first part, and the specific examples of the second, you are ready to move forward against your own challenges.

The challenges are there. They're real, they're deadly, and they've always been borne by those who shoulder the warrior's burdens. This book has brought you up to the Line of Departure but that's as far as it can go. From here on out, it's up to you.

So, muster your knowledge, decide upon your plan, and step out with confidence. The only way to fail is to quit trying.

EPILOGUE

THOSE WHO'VE FOUGHT in Iraq and Afghanistan have an historic opportunity to redefine the veteran's experience for future generations of American warriors. How? By approaching the challenges of coming home as integral components of the warrior's journey, not as aberrations that only affect the weak.

America's relationship with her veterans has matured to a point where invisible wounds are socially understood to be unavoidable consequences of sending troops to war. It is time we, as veterans, do the same. The reality of combat has changed each and every one of us in fundamental ways. If we take the opportunity afforded us by the current political and social atmosphere to understand these changes, we stand to become better men and women, fathers and mothers, brothers and sisters, husbands and wives, friends, and citizens.

This opportunity did not happen overnight. It was created by the tireless efforts of generations of American veterans—past and present. The warriors who came before us labored long and hard to secure the social, political, and economic support we enjoy today. Lest we take this support for granted, we should remember that America has not always been so inclined to care for those who fight her wars. Consider these facts, catalogued in James Wright's excellent work, *Those Who Have Borne the Battle:*

> —1783: Congress refuses to fund pensions already promised to Continental Army officers for service during the Revolutionary War. A coup by Continental Army officers is narrowly avoided by George Washington's personal intervention. (p.25)

— In reaction to petitions from individual veterans with claims of Revolutionary War related injuries, the Congressional Committee on Claims stated: "Congress cannot undertake the support of paupers merely because they may have been at some period of their lives engaged in the public service." (p.67)

—"No uniform pension for all surviving members of the War of 1812 existed until 1871 . . ." (p.76)

—"Congress approved comprehensive pensions for all [1846] Mexican War veterans in 1887." (p.77)

—In 1932 a group of some 20,000 veterans and their families assembled in Washington DC to petition the government for early payment of a bonus promised to veterans of WWI. Army Chief of Staff Douglas MacArthur ". . . personally led mounted cavalry commanded by George Patton, tanks, and infantry with tear-gas canisters and bayonets to expel the veterans." (p.93)

Take a look at how far we've come. In 1932, in the worst of the Depression, *our own military, under orders from the President, attacked veterans with tanks, bayonets, and tear-gas* because they were asking for early payment of an already agreed upon bonus. Contrast that with the fact that, in 2014, a scandal concerning *wait times* at the Phoenix Veterans Affairs Medical Center ignited a public outcry that resulted in the resignation of VA Secretary Shinseki less than two months later. A month after that, President Obama signed a bill into law appropriating an additional $16 billion to overhaul the VA.

Bayonets and tanks on one hand, accountability and more

money on the other. These two examples show the evolution of America's relationship with her veterans and highlight the importance and primacy of veterans' affairs in current political dialogues.

Far from having to scrabble for pensions and bonuses, today's veterans have a wealth of opportunities waiting for them. Want to go to school? The Post 9-11 GI Bill is there to pay for it. How about starting your own business? The Small Business Administration has a whole department dedicated to helping veterans accomplish this. Need a house loan? Veterans are eligible for those as well. Medical care remains a challenge for veterans, but, given the disarray of our healthcare system as a whole, that problem is not limited to VA facilities.

Even though challenges remain, the benefits available to today's veterans are wide-ranging and comprehensive. Perhaps even more importantly, they are provided ungrudgingly by the vast majority of society. These benefits are not considered as gifts to be doled out or withdrawn at will, but rather as a national obligation to those few Americans who choose to serve.

The organization directly responsible for fulfilling this national obligation is far from perfect. But as a governmental bureaucracy, the VA has demonstrated laudable willingness to address internal shortcomings and is making honest efforts to correct them—even if its feet must be held to the fire to do it. And with veteran service organizations and organized veterans' groups wielding increasing political power, the problems at the VA are being corrected faster than ever before.

But improving veterans' reintegration will take more than just fixing the VA. It will require changes in how we as a nation view the human costs of sending men and women to war. These adjustments have to occur on multiple levels: from the individual veteran's understanding of how their experiences changed them, to the political wisdom to consider *all* the costs of conflict before engaging, to American society's sharing of the burdens they've asked their military to assume in their name.

Most of those changes are beyond our ability to influence directly. Changing American society and injecting wisdom into political discourse are difficult, if not impossible, for most veterans to accomplish on their own. The improvements in those areas will take years of gradual adjustments if they happen at all.

But there is one area where each and every veteran can have a direct impact: the individual level. If we accept the concept that our duties as warriors do not end until we've met the challenges of coming home, then we stand to positively impact the reintegration of all veterans—now and in the future. Once we've done the hard work to process and learn from our own experiences, then we are in a position to apply our hard-earned wisdom to any number of political, social, and cultural problems. In this manner, the successful return of one veteran can be multiplied thousands of times as he or she shares their boon with their circle of influence, however large or small it may be.

This bottom-up approach has been overlooked in the current national dialogue about veterans. This is likely because few are willing to say that *veterans have the ultimate responsibility to navigate the challenges of coming home.* Others are willing to help, but each and every one of us has to be the driving force behind our own successful return. There is no other way.

This book draws heavily from my own experiences to illuminate a pathway through the challenges of coming home, but my path is not the only one that exists. You may find different tools to use and different routes to take and, indeed, I hope you do. If this book does no more than spark conversations between veterans who measure my efforts and find them ineffective against their own, then I will consider it an unqualified success. It would be the open sharing of what worked for them, and the fact that the conversation happened at all, that would signal progress for veterans as a whole.

Our service to the nation did not end when we took off our uniforms. By spreading out through society as healthy, well-adjusted veterans, we stand to influence not only our immediate family and friends with our wisdom and maturity, but also the fortunes of the nation as a whole. Crisis and conflict will always be part of our world, and future generations of American men and women—our children—will have to deal with them. Rest assured, they'll shoulder the burdens of service and take the fight to our enemies, just like we did. Then they'll come home and realize their challenges are not over, just like we did. The military will teach them what they need to know to fight and win. It will be up to us to teach them how to fully come home. The only way we can do that is if we've done it ourselves.

CONCLUSION

THE WARRIOR'S JOURNEY—the hero's journey—is nothing more than a label placed on the particular branch of human consciousness that has carried strong men and women through life-changing experiences since the dawn of time. This book has tried to explain how this current influences your life and how you can better navigate its twists and turns by becoming an active participant instead of a passive observer.

What lies at the end of this journey? Well, death. That's because the warrior's journey continues for as long as you live. It's a circle you'll pass through many times in your life on slightly different trajectories. If you develop and maintain the self-awareness borne of honest introspection, the challenges of each revolution will teach you different valuable lessons, and you'll continue to grow in maturity and wisdom. By refusing to stagnate, you stand to live a meaningful, fulfilled life surrounded by people who love and cherish you—faults and all.

It is my sincere hope that your life as a veteran is consciously guided by what you've learned from your experiences in uniform. Hard lessons about the value and fragility of life, often written in the blood of our heroes, should never be forgotten.

If nothing else matters to you, think about this. When you do die, when you finally link-up with your buddies who fell in battle, how do you want them to greet you? Will they shake their heads at how you pissed away the opportunities they were denied? Will they berate you for remaining mired in the past and ruining your chances for happiness?

Or will they greet you with a proud smile and a chest-crushing embrace? When the thudding, closed-fisted, back-pounding is done and the tears self-consciously wiped away, will they take a step back, hold you at arms length and say:

You did good, real good.

I don't know. But that's what I'm going for.

ACKNOWLEDGEMENTS

Throughout the writing of this book, I have received assistance from numerous sources—from my own VA counselor to fellow veterans and my entire family. Key through it all has been my editor and friend, David Hazard, Director of Ascent. His guidance provided the structure upon which to hang my arguments and observations. Without his efforts, this book would never have escaped my cluttered mind.

I must also thank the many "test-readers" who suffered through early drafts of the manuscript and whose feedback helped me avoid critical mistakes and omissions: Major General Tom Jones, USMC (Ret), Mike Young, Deborah Humphreys, Dave Humphreys, Eric Potterat, Charlie Panten, Larry Tritle, Steve Fiscus, Isaac Lee, Jenn Marino, and Ken Falke. Thank you all for taking time out of your busy schedules to make this book better.

Special thanks is due to Dr. Jonathan Shay. His books traced the symptoms of combat trauma through *The Iliad* and *The Odyssey* and opened my eyes to the normalcy of my own reactions to combat. As if that wasn't enough, his gracious willingness to help edit the final version of this book, and write its Foreword, greatly increased its value to veterans of all conflicts and traumas. Thank you, Jonathan.

Once again the task of correcting my convoluted prose and nonsensical usage of apostrophes and commas fell to the best proofreading team out there—my mother and sister. If any mistakes remain, it's because I ignored their advice.

To my wonderful children—thank you for that one time you watched TV quietly so I could work. Now, stop hitting each other.

And to my beautiful wife, Lena: Thank you for giving me the opportunity to continue writing. If it does someday pay the bills, you can retire, my dear. I promise.

BIBLIOGRAPHY

Campbell, Joseph. *The Hero with a Thousand Faces*. New World Library, 2008.

Campbell, Joseph. *The Power of Myth*. MJF Books, 1988.

Childers, Thomas. *Soldier from the War Returning: The Greatest Generation's Troubled Homecoming from World War II*. Mariner Books, 2010.

Colman, Andrew M. *Oxford Dictionary of Psychology*. Oxford University Press, 2009.

Gabriel, Richard. *No More Heroes: Madness & Psychiatry in War*. Hill and Wang, 1987.

Herman, Judith Lewis. *Trauma and Recovery: The Aftermath of Violence—from Domestic Abuse to Political Terror*. Basic Books, 1997.

Hoge, Col. Charles. *Once a Warrior—Always a Warrior: Navigating the Transition from Combat to Home*. Lyons Press, 2010.

Holm, Tom. *Strong Hearts, Wounded Souls: Native American Veterans of the Vietnam War*. University of Texas Press, 1996.

Parker, Kim. 2011. "The Military-Civilian Gap: Fewer Family Connections." 23 November, 2011. http:/www.pewso-cialtrends.org.

Meyers, Dakota, and Bing West. *Into the Fire: A Firsthand Account of the Most Extraordinary Battle in the Afghan War*. Random House, 2012.

Shay, Jonathan. *Achilles in Vietnam: Combat Trauma and the Undoing of Character*. Simon & Schuster, 1995.

Shay, Jonathan. *Odysseus in America: Combat Trauma and the Trials of Homecoming*. Scribner, 2003.

Tick, Edward. *War and the Soul: Healing Our Nation's Veterans from Post-Traumatic Stress Disorder*. Quest Books, 2005.

Wright, James. *Those Who Have Borne the Battle: A History of America's Wars and Those Who Fought Them*. PublicAffairs, 2012.

ADDITIONAL SUGGESTED READING

Delaney, Bob, and Dave Scheiber. *Surviving the Shadows: A Journey of Hope into Post-Traumatic Stress.* Sourcebooks, 2011.

Frankl, Viktor E. *Man's Search for Meaning.* Buccaneer Books, 1992.

Grossman, Lt.Col. Dave. *On Killing: The Psychological Cost of Learning to Kill in War and Society.* Back Bay Books/Little, Brown and Company, 2009.

Leeming, David. *The Oxford Companion to World Mythology.* Oxford University Press, 2005.

Lifton, Robert Jay. *Home from the War.* Simon & Schuster, 1973.

Marlantes, Karl. *What It Is Like to Go to War.* Grove Press, 2011.

Sheehan, Dan. *After Action: The True Story of a Cobra Pilot's Journey.* CreateSpace, 2012.

Tick, Edward. *Warrior's Return: Restoring the Soul After War.* Sounds True, 2014.

Verkamp, Bernard. *The Moral Treatment of Returning Warriors in Early Medieval and Modern Times.* University of Scranton Press, 2006.

APPENDIX A

DE-COMPARTMENTALIZATION CHECKLIST

Gather the Intel.

- Locate anything you wrote during your deployments.

- Letters and e-mails home—Ask family and friends for copies of anything you sent them while you were deployed.

- Debrief notes from missions

- Personal journals: yours, your buddy's, etc.

- Official history of your unit(s) (see Appendix B for Points of Contact)

Using a calendar, write significant events on the dates they occurred.

- Deployment dates

- Major firefights or operations

- Injuries or wounds—self and buddies

- Holidays

- Rest and Relaxation leave

- Anything noteworthy mentioned in material from Section 1

- Seemingly insignificant events if they pop up in your memory

Using a 3-ring binder or notebook, record all the facts associated with events on your calendar, giving each event at least one full sheet of paper.

Record underneath the date:
- Who, what, when, where, why for each event

- Any information associated with that event that pops up in your memory

- Any emotions you experience in relation to that event, both current and remembered

- Any physical reactions to the event, both current and remembered

Use the information recorded in your notebook/3-ring binder to write your narrative

Starting with the first significant event recorded, link emotions and facts together to tell your story about each event. Use new notebook.

- Writing will take as much time as needed.

- Don't rush or become frustrated if progress seems slow.

- Seek out buddy- and corpsman-aid if desired.

- Writing workshops

- Veterans writing groups

- VA writing therapy programs

Verify the narrative is true.

- Once complete, don't look at your narrative for a while.

- Allow your mind to clear—could take days, weeks, months.

- Reread the narrative and make note of anything that rings false or triggers your "bullshit" warning.

- Rework flagged portions of the narrative.

- Repeat the "clear, reread, rework" cycle as many times as necessary until you feel you got it right.

Share the narrative with a trustworthy listener. Choose your mode of communication.

- Choose your mode of communication.

- Visual art—painting, photography, sculpture, etc.

- Music

- Dance

- Writing

- Anything else that allows you to adequately communicate

- Start small.

- Initially, share with intimate friends, close family.

- Expand the size of the audience, if you desire, as you become comfortable sharing.

Record and reflect upon any realizations you come to while sharing.

APPENDIX B

POINTS OF CONTACT
FOR OFFICIAL UNIT HISTORIES

U.S. Air Force Historical Research Agency
600 Chennault Circle
Maxwell AFB, AL 36112-6424
Telephone: (334) 953-2395

U.S. Army Center of Military History
102 4th Avenue, Bldg 35
Fort McNair, DC 20319-5060
Telephone: (202) 685-4042
www.history.army.mil

U.S. Naval History & Heritage Command
Washington Navy Yard, Bldg 57 (3rd Floor)
Washington, DC 20374
Telephone: (202) 433-3224

U.S. Marine Corps History Division
3078 Upshur Avenue
Quantico, Virginia 22134
Telephone: (703) 432-4877

U.S. Coast Guard Historian's Office
Commandant (CG-09224)
ATTN: Historian's Office
U.S. Coast Guard Stop 7031
2703 Martin Luther King, Jr. Ave. SE
Washington, DC 20593-7039
Telephone: (202)-372-4651

APPENDIX C

LIST OF USEFUL WEBSITES AND PHONE NUMBERS

This short list provides starting points for you to research various self-, buddy-, and corpsman-aid options.

Corpsman/Medic-Aid

Vet Center: http://www.vetcenter.va.gov

Vet Center Combat Call Center: 1-877-WAR-VETS (1-877-927-8387)

Veterans Crisis Line: http://www.veteranscrisisline.net (1-800-273-8255)

Buddy-Aid

World T.E.A.M Sports: http://worldteamsports.org
   *Check out their "Resources" page for links to various sporting organizations specifically oriented toward veterans.

GallantFew Revolutionary Veteran Support Network: http://www.gallantfew.org

Iraq Afghanistan Veterans of America: http://iava.org

Veterans of Foreign Wars: http://www.vfw.org

Arts/Writing

Veterans Writing Project: http://veteranswriting.org

Warrior Writers: http://www.warriorwriters.org

Foundation for Art & Healing: http://www.artandhealing.org

Operation We Are Here: http://www.operationwearehere.com/MusicTherapy.html
   *Check out their "Therapeutic Opportunities" page for links to nonprofits providing instruments and lessons to veterans.